INQUIRY INTO THE
COLLEGE
CLASSROOM

INQUIRY INTO THE COLLEGE CLASSROOM

A JOURNEY TOWARD SCHOLARLY TEACHING

Paul Savory
Amy Nelson Burnett
Amy Goodburn

UNIVERSITY OF NEBRASKA-LINCOLN

ANKER PUBLISHING COMPANY, INC.
Bolton, Massachusetts

Inquiry Into the College Classroom
A Journey Toward Scholarly Teaching

ISBN 978-1-933371-25-2

Composition and cover design by Dutton & Sherman Design

Anker Publishing Company, Inc.
563 Main Street
P.O. Box 249
Bolton, MA 01740-0249 USA

www.ankerpub.com

Library of Congress Cataloging-in-Publication Data

Savory, Paul.
  Inquiry into the college classroom : a journey toward scholarly teaching / Paul Savory, Amy Nelson Burnett, Amy Goodburn.
      p. cm.
  Includes bibliographical references and index.
  ISBN 978-1-933371-25-2
  1. College teaching—United States. I. Burnett, Amy Nelson, 1957.
II. Goodburn, Amy M. III. Title.

  LB2331.S28 2007
  378.1'2—dc22   2006102500

TABLE OF CONTENTS

LIST OF EXHIBITS

ABOUT THE AUTHORS

IN ADDITION TO HAVING co-written the book *Making Teaching and Learning Visible: Course Portfolios and the Peer Review of Teaching* (Anker, 2006), the three authors coordinate the University of Nebraska–Lincoln's (UNL) Peer Review of Teaching Project.

Paul Savory is an associate professor in the Department of Industrial and Management Systems Engineering at the University of Nebraska–Lincoln. He earned his Ph.D. from Arizona State University in 1993. His teaching and research interests include engineering education, discrete-event computer simulation, engineering management, statistics, and operations research. He has received numerous department, college, and university awards for his teaching effectiveness, the most recent being the UNL Hollings Family Engineering Educator Award. In 2003, he was inducted into the UNL Academy of Distinguished Teachers.

Amy Nelson Burnett is professor of history at the University of Nebraska–Lincoln. She received her Ph.D. in early modern European history from the University of Wisconsin–Madison in 1989. She is the author of *Teaching the Reformation: Ministers and Their Message in Basel, 1529–1629* (Oxford University Press, 2006) and *The Yoke of Christ: Martin Bucer and Christian Discipline* (Truman State University Press, 1994), as well as numerous articles and essays on the Protestant Reformation in southern

Germany and Switzerland. She is the recipient of a Research Fellowship from the Alexander von Humboldt Foundation and has taught at the University of Hannover in Germany. In 1999, she received a College of Arts and Sciences Distinguished Teaching Award.

 *Amy Goodburn* is associate dean of the College of Arts and Sciences and associate professor of English and women's and gender studies at the University of Nebraska–Lincoln. She received her Ph.D. in English from The Ohio State University in 1994. She teaches courses in writing, rhetoric, and literacy studies. Her research focuses on ethnographic and teacher research, multicultural pedagogies, and curriculum development. Her recent edited collection is *Composition, Pedagogy, and the Scholarship of Teaching* (Boynton/Cook, 2002). Her contributions to teaching have been recognized with a College of Arts and Sciences Distinguished Teaching Award, the UNL Scholarly Teaching Award, and induction into the UNL Academy of Distinguished Teachers.

ACKNOWLEDGMENTS

THIS BOOK COULD NOT have been written without the contributions of a great many people, and we are deeply indebted to each of them.

- *For allowing us to make public their classroom inquiry work:* Tom Berg, Carolyn Edwards, Dana Fritz, Frauke Hachtmann, Elizabeth Ingraham, Kevin Lee, B. D'Andra Orey, Tim Wentz, and Gordon Woodward.
- *For supporting (and funding) our University of Nebraska–Lincoln Peer Review of Teaching Project and offering invaluable advice, praise, and motivation when needed:* UNL administrators and faculty David Wilson (Associate Vice Chancellor for Academic Affairs), Rita Kean (Dean of the Office of Undergraduate Studies), Richard Edwards (Professor of Economics and former Senior Vice Chancellor for Academic Affairs) and Barbara Couture (Senior Vice Chancellor for Academic Affairs).
- *For working with our campus faculty to document their teaching:* Whitney Douglas.

Finally, a special thanks to Daniel Bernstein, professor of psychology and director of the Center for Teaching Excellence at the University of Kansas. Dan started the Peer Review of Teaching Project on our campus, involved each of us as a project participant, and later brought each of us onboard to help run the project. Since he left for the University of Kansas in 2002, we have built on the excellent foundation he laid to create a program that supports faculty as they document, share, and evaluate the intellectual work of their teaching. Thank you, Dan. Our efforts would not have been possible without your assistance, guidance, and years of hard work.

CHAPTER ONE

A GUIDE FOR SCHOLARLY INQUIRY INTO TEACHING

WHAT IS HAPPENING IN MY CLASSROOM?

As COLLEGE TEACHERS, we constantly ask ourselves questions about our classroom practices and our students' learning:

- How can I help students work more effectively in groups?
- Can I change students' perceptions by teaching a certain topic in a different way?
- Will converting all my lectures to PowerPoint presentations improve student learning?
- What is the effect of having external speakers come talk to my class?
- Will changing my examinations from multiple-choice questions to essay questions improve my students' critical thinking skills?

These questions are only a small sample of those that might occur to us before, during, and after each course that we teach. We often attempt to answer such questions using the evidence we have—student remarks during class and office hours, student performance on examinations or homework assignments, student comments solicited via teaching evaluations, and our own classroom observations. While these forms of evidence can be useful, such informal assessments can also be misleading, particularly because they are generally not systematic or fully representative. For instance, having one student during office hours say she "hated watching the classroom PowerPoint presentations" might bias your perception of their usefulness, even if the other students in the course benefited from them but never voiced their opinions. *How, then, can you carry out a more systematic inquiry into your teaching and your students' learning? How can you develop methods and processes for truly finding out what improves student learning in your courses?*

You probably were introduced to disciplinary-based research methods through advanced coursework or faculty mentoring. You thus know that the quality of the result is influenced by how you ask a research question and what methodology you use to answer it. The same is true for an inquiry into your classroom. Yet few of us have been taught how to frame inquiry questions for our teaching, and we are often left to struggle on our own. For this reason, it is useful to have a guide to follow when we examine our teaching practices and reflect on their effectiveness in improving student learning.

This book will help you formalize a process for developing and testing an inquiry question in your classroom. This process is intended to help you gather and evaluate a range of information concerning your teaching—measuring the effectiveness of a specific classroom technique or a certain type of assessment, or addressing broader questions related to course structure and emphasis—and assess its impact on student learning. Our goal, shared by Walvoord and Anderson (1998), is to help you approach your own teaching in a more structured fashion, as you investigate teaching questions that you really care about, that cycle back into your teaching for improved student learning, that are embedded within a specific classroom context, and that you may have encountered over successive course offerings.

You do not need to become an educational researcher in order to approach your classroom in this way. We all face the time pressures of teaching courses and of remaining current in our own disciplines, and we can't be expected to develop yet another area of expertise that bears little practical relation to our teaching and research responsibilities. In contrast to disciplinary-based research, classroom inquiry has very practical outcomes for those teaching in other disciplines. Not only will it help you to answer those persistent questions you have about student learning, but it also will help you to improve subsequent offerings of a course and/or streamline the process of designing future courses. Your inquiry will make your teaching easier as you develop a better sense of what does and does not work in your classroom. And, if you wish, you can also make your inquiry results available to others for use, discussion, and review.

TEACHING: A SCHOLARLY JOURNEY

Ernest Boyer's seminal work *Scholarship Reconsidered: Priorities of the Professoriate* (1990) sought to broaden the definition of scholarship to include the scholarship of teaching. Since its publication, *Scholarship Reconsidered* has generated numerous debates and discussions within the higher education community about what the scholarship of teaching is and how it can be assessed. Organizations and initiatives such as the Carnegie Foundation for the Advancement of Teaching and Learning, the Peer Review of Teaching Project, and the Visible Knowledge Project have all offered various models for promoting inquiry into teaching and representing the intellectual work of one's teaching in different forms. Glassick, Huber, and Maeroff (1997) suggest that the six criteria typically used for evaluating faculty research (clear goals, adequate preparation, appropriate methods, significant results, effective presentation, and reflective critique) can also be used to read and assess teaching as scholarship. Yet teaching is seldom conceptualized in this way. In his often-cited article, "The Scholarship of Teaching: What's the Problem?," Randy Bass (1999) contrasts the situation in research, where a problem is "at the heart of the investigative process . . . around which all creative and productive activity revolves," with that of teaching, where a problem is "something you don't want to have, and if you have one, you probably want to fix it" (p. 1).

In response to this disparity between how problems in teaching and research are conceptualized, the scholarship of teaching movement encourages teachers to approach challenging questions concerning their teaching with the same critical intellectual energy that they use when conducting their disciplinary research. This shift in thinking about one's teaching requires moving beyond anecdotal or informal measures of inquiry to a more structured examination of teaching and of student learning. The inquiry model presented in this chapter will help you approach your teaching with these criteria in mind. The subsequent nine chapters of this book highlight actual examples of teachers performing classroom inquiry on a wide range of questions. These examples will provide you with guides to what other teachers have done and illustrate a variety of approaches and methods for classroom inquiry. While the course content of these inquiries might be far afield of your own discipline, the questions these teachers ask and the methods that they use to investigate them are similar to what you face regardless of your disciplinary expertise. So whether you teach physics or English, anthropology or nursing, we think you will find that many of these inquiry examples resonate with your own teaching experience and interest. The final chapter offers advice on getting started with your own classroom inquiry, discusses in more detail the types of resources available to you, and describes the networks of teachers who are engaged in similar inquiry into teaching.

As you adopt a more formal procedure for inquiry into your classroom, you will begin a journey toward becoming a *scholarly teacher*. We use the word *journey* to describe this process since it implies that you will plan and prepare for your trip, you will move from one point to another, and you will ultimately arrive at your intended destination. In becoming a scholarly teacher, you move from an informal inquiry process to a more formal approach to examining your teaching and the student learning that results. Common characteristics of a scholarly teacher include (Glassick et al., 1997):

- Remaining current in your disciplinary or content knowledge area
- Learning about different teaching styles and approaches
- Improving student learning within your own classroom by investigating the impact of your teaching on your students
- Improving student learning within your local community (department, college, school) through collecting, sharing, and communicating the results of your work on teaching and learning

Scholarly teachers use reflection, inquiry, testing, and evaluation to examine and improve their own teaching, to increase their students' learning, and to contribute to broader conversations about teaching at their school.

Those who continue on the journey of scholarly teaching may arrive at what is commonly termed the *scholarship of teaching and learning* or *SoTL*, in which postsecondary teachers work toward the goal of valuing and rewarding inquiry into teaching commensurate with that of disciplinary-based scholarship. Lee Shulman (1998) has observed that "for an activity to be designated as scholarship, it should manifest at least three key characteristics: It should be public, susceptible to critical review and evaluation, and accessible for exchange and use by other members of one's scholarly community" (p. 5). While it is difficult to draw exact distinctions, SoTL researchers differ from scholarly teachers by:

- Knowing and citing the literature on teaching and learning
- Relating the literature on teaching and learning to discipline-specific questions and issues
- Publishing and sharing their work to disciplinary or teaching

community audiences to expand discussions on teaching and student learning

While deeper engagement with the literature and broader contact with teachers from other schools may benefit your teaching, involvement in SoTL research is not for everyone. We have found that while some faculty find SoTL work central to their professional lives, others are content to be scholarly teachers in less public ways.

The journey toward scholarly teaching leads in many different directions, and you can use classroom inquiry to reach whatever teaching destination you set for yourself. Most teachers engage in classroom inquiry primarily to improve their teaching methods and practices so that they can increase and document student learning. Consider this comment from a professor of art on how documenting and understanding her students' learning in and of itself has been empowering and professionally satisfying:

> Following the classroom inquiry model gave me a framework in which to refine my course. Although the methods I used seemed at first too scientific for a subjective area like art, the "Hypothesis, Data, Conclusion" structure allowed me to be more objective about my teaching. In doing so, it has helped me to write better curricula and more fairly evaluate student learning. The reflective writing process used to develop my classroom inquiry was so useful that it inspired me to assign my students to reflect in writing on their own drawing process and progress. Among other things, this written component helps me to better understand their perceptions of the course and helps students to see their progress more clearly.

While most journeys have their share of excitement, they might also present difficulties or offer opportunities for alternate routes. Our inquiry model helps prepare you for these difficulties by being flexible enough to allow for detours along the way.

One of the crucial activities in exploring a classroom inquiry question is writing reflective commentary that documents your teaching journey. Writing reflectively about your course allows you to begin to make sense of your pedagogical decisions and their impact on classroom practices, student behaviors, attitudes, perceptions, and overall student learning. Indeed, there are a number of educators who study "reflective practice." Brookfield (1995) notes:

Theorists of reflective practice are interested in helping teachers understand, question, investigate, and take seriously their own learning and practice. Some of the many benefits teachers gain from critically reflecting on their teaching include 1) taking more informed actions, 2) developing rationales for practices, 3) avoiding self-blame when teaching goes awry, and 4) grounding us in the reality of our classrooms. (p. 215)

By documenting your classroom inquiry through writing, you will develop artifacts that demonstrate your effectiveness as a teacher and that provide an evidence-based account of your scholarly journey. In addition, writing about the process will enable you to assess the value of teaching practices that thus far you may have taken for granted and to see the quality of your teaching and students' learning in new ways. Exhibit 1.1 lists other possible uses for documenting a classroom inquiry (Bernstein, Burnett, Goodburn, & Savory, 2006).

Exhibit 1.1
Uses of Classroom Inquiry Work

- Developing a new course
- Summarizing your teaching for annual merit review evaluations
- Supporting teaching award applications
- Documenting and assessing your faculty development efforts
- Highlighting your teaching as part of a promotion and tenure packet
- Structuring or showcasing a curricular revision
- Aiding in a department program review
- Supporting a job application
- Providing or assessing learning outcomes for department or program accreditation

---

A MODEL FOR YOUR CLASSROOM INQUIRY

The inquiry model that we share is not new—it mirrors the approach one typically applies to disciplinary-based scholarly research. As teachers, we expect our students to be able to record, demonstrate, and explain their results. In the same vein, your reflective writing about your classroom inquiry can be used and shared with others, providing the basis for discussions about teaching that move beyond the anecdotal or passing hallway conversations with colleagues. The significant difference is that the subject you are studying is more personal, because you are examining yourself as a teacher and the impact of your decisions and actions on your students' learning. Traditionally the classroom has been viewed as a private space, but we suggest that opening one's classroom for inquiry—and making such inquiry public—often leads to improved teaching and enhanced student learning.

In general, there are four major steps to carrying out an effective classroom inquiry: formulating an inquiry question, developing an assessment strategy, evaluating the results of your study, and drawing conclusions and recommendations from those results. Following a formal model improves and simplifies the inquiry process by preventing false starts, keeping you focused on your question, helping you determine the most effective means of answering that question, and allowing you to generalize your conclusions so that they apply to other teachers or to different learning situations. Exhibit 1.2 presents some common pitfalls that result when teachers do not use a formal process or model of inquiry.

Exhibit 1.2
Common Pitfalls of Informal Inquiry

- Collecting unnecessary data in the hope of making some sense of it afterward
- Attempting to fit meaningful inquiry questions to existing but insufficient classroom data
- Failing to recognize limitations in your inquiry that restrict the range of your conclusions and their applicability to other teaching situations
- Overlooking alternative explanations or hypotheses for a given set of classroom findings

---

The steps we discuss will guide you through the process of formalized classroom inquiry. At first glance, our model may seem overly structured or too detailed, but don't be intimidated or overwhelmed by it. Tourist guidebooks generally describe all the attractions in a particular area and even prescribe exact routes to follow. Tourists completely unfamiliar with an area may appreciate the detail and want to visit everything, while those more familiar with the region may pick and choose what they want to see and prefer to follow alternate routes. In the same way, we have made explicit all the elements that can be included in a classroom inquiry and have outlined a sequence to follow for that inquiry. Our steps are intended to help individuals at all stages of their scholarly journey, and so we have made each step as complete as possible. Those just beginning this journey may want to follow our model step by step. Others may already be employing some of the elements of scholarly teaching and so might want to expand on certain parts of the model and omit others. In all cases, though, you should feel free to adapt our model to fit your own goals and purposes for pursuing inquiry into your teaching.

INQUIRY STEP 1
Reflecting on Course Background, History, and Development

To get started, it is useful to write an overview of your course, describing its history, goals, place in the broader curriculum, and institutional context. While you are probably well aware of these details, writing them out can help you to highlight and make explicit your classroom and learning issues and concerns. For instance, perhaps outside influences (accreditation requirements, program goals, external audiences) affect your development of course goals and expectations of student learning outcomes. Writing about these influences might help you to better understand what you can and cannot control in your course or to identify a question that will allow you to investigate more fully the tensions these influences might cause. Your description of the course will also allow future readers of your work to put your classroom inquiry into a larger context. Exhibit 1.3 offers prompts to help you describe your course.

EXHIBIT 1.3
Prompts for Putting Your Course in Context

Major Question	*Possible Items to Highlight*
What is your course?	What is your course about? What is the content area covered? Who are your students (e.g., first, second, third, fourth year, graduate, majors or nonmajors)? What sorts of backgrounds do students bring to your course? How does your course fit into your departmental curriculum? Does it fit into curricula in other departments? Does your course lay the foundation for courses that follow it or build on what students have already learned in other courses?

What are your goals for the course?	What do you want students to know? What do you want them to be able to do? What do you want them to understand? What do you want them to retain from your course? What perspectives or attitudes do you want them to develop? What is important for them to learn about your field? How do your goals fit in with the goals of other courses in your department or discipline? What should they learn about themselves as students or as contributors to society?
What is the course history?	How long have you been teaching this course? What role have you played in developing it?
How has the course evolved?	How has the course changed over successive offerings (in terms of course goals, assignments, pedagogical strategies, etc.)? Why have you made those changes, and how have they influenced student learning?

INQUIRY STEP 2
Identifying an Issue to Investigate

Once you have sketched out the history of your course, your next task is to write about the issues or problems posed in the course that you would like to explore. We suggest that you select a problem that engages your attention and begs for a solution. Again, we are using the term *problem* here in the positive sense that Bass (1999) gives it: as an investigative possibility rather than as something negative that needs to be "fixed." If you already have a specific issue in mind, you can immediately go to the next inquiry step. But if you are like most teachers, you might be a bit more perplexed or uncertain about what you should investigate. In this case, reflecting on those classroom issues that concern you will help you narrow your inquiry to what is most important. While all classroom inquiries ultimately concern student learning, you can approach most questions about what and how well your students learn from two directions:

- *Focusing on the outcome:* a specific type of student learning and development
- *Focusing on the procedure:* a specific instructional activity or practice

Building on the category definitions of Cerbin and Kopp (2004), Exhibit 1.4 offers a range of inquiry questions that you might explore.

EXHIBIT 1.4
Examples of Classroom Questions

Type of Inquiry	Example Inquiry Question
Idea development	How does student understanding of a particular concept or topic develop or change during the term?
Range of understanding	Is student learning different for various subsets or classifications of students in the course? Example: majors vs. nonmajors, males vs. females, undergraduate students vs. graduate students
Depth of understanding	How much content knowledge and understanding are students gaining from the course in comparison to their knowledge before the course? Can they apply concepts to a situation or merely state the definition of a concept?
Misconceptions	What misconceptions are students bringing to the course and how do these misconceptions change as a result of the course?
Understanding difficult ideas	How do students develop an understanding of particularly difficult course concepts?
Long-term learning	As a result of your course, what knowledge or long-term skills will students carry into other courses and into their careers?
Transfer of learning	Are students able to demonstrate understanding and application of the course concepts in a later course for which this course is a prerequisite?
Measure of critical thinking	Can students interpret, understand, process, and apply the course concepts to new situations?
Progressive dialogue	How does students' understanding develop from classroom and/or online discussions?
Instructional practice	What is the impact of a specific teaching method, course activity, or course material on students' learning?

Once you have selected an issue that is significant to you, it is useful to reflect on the importance of this issue in terms of how it has affected your teaching and your students' learning. Probing this connection can help you to further articulate the scope of the issue. You might find that what you originally identified as a key issue is really a subset of a larger question. Or, conversely, you might find this process useful in identifying a smaller component that is really the central issue you want to examine. Exhibit 1.5 offers useful prompts as you write about the issue you wish to address in your course.

EXHIBIT 1.5
Prompts for Describing an Issue in Your Course

Major Question	Possible Items to Highlight
What is an issue or problem you hope to study in your course?	Why is it useful or important for you as a teacher to investigate this problem? How might investigating this issue contribute to your students' learning, your own professional development, and/or the scholarship of teaching in your field?
What does the issue look like in your course?	When did you first observe this issue/problem? What are some causes of or explanations for this issue (e.g., student preparation, curricular fragmentation, teacher experience, institutional context)? Have you taken any steps to address the issue already? If so, what were these steps and what were the outcomes? (If you have sought to address this issue over successive course offerings, provide a timeline or sequence of modifications that you have made to address the issue.)
Is this issue/problem directly addressed within the course?	Are there readings, assignments, or course activities through which students engage with this issue/problem? Describe the ideal outcome(s) you believe would be achieved if this issue were addressed or solved within this particular course.

As you narrow your focus, it is also important to consider your own ability to carry out an inquiry concerning the issue. Since you are probably not conversant with all the tools necessary to conduct statistically pure classroom research (if such pure classroom research even exists!), you need to assess whether you are truly prepared to inquire into the issue you have identified. Exhibit 1.6 offers some detailed questions to help you assess your issue and your ability to answer it. If you envision sharing or publishing your classroom inquiry, Exhibit 1.7 lists questions that are applicable to preparing your work for external audiences.

Exhibit 1.6
Self-Evaluation Questions on the Practicality of Studying the Issue

- Will my inquiry lead to improved teaching and student learning?
- Am I interested in this issue/problem yet free from strong bias so that I can study it objectively?
- Do I possess or can I acquire the necessary skills, abilities, and/or background to study the problem?
- Do I have access to the tools, equipment, or laboratories necessary to conduct the inquiry?
- Have I framed an issue or problem that can be productively studied during a single term (e.g., semester, quarter) of the course?
- Can I obtain adequate data?
- Can I obtain administrative support, guidance, and cooperation for conducting my inquiry?
- Will the findings be of practical value to myself and other teachers?

Exhibit 1.7
Self-Evaluation Questions on the Appeal to External Audiences

- Will my inquiry advance my (and others') knowledge?
- Will the findings be of practical value to other teachers?
- Will my inquiry duplicate the work that has been or is being done adequately by someone else?
- If this topic has been covered, does my inquiry extend it beyond its present form?
- Will my classroom inquiry lead to the development of other investigations?

INQUIRY STEP 3
Defining an Inquiry Hypothesis

Now that you have identified an important issue to study, you have laid the foundation for your classroom inquiry. There is a well-known saying that "a question well stated is a question half answered." Developing an inquiry hypothesis for your issue clarifies what you are going to do and provides a path for answering it. A hypothesis can take the form of a conditional statement ("More frequent recitation sections will improve students' test scores") or an if-then statement ("If I have more frequent recitation sessions, students' test scores will improve"). In most cases, though, it is easiest to develop and then test a hypothesis that is framed as a question ("Will more frequent recitation sessions improve students' test scores?").

A well-defined inquiry hypothesis can have up to four major components:

- *A subject group:* Who or what are you interested in studying?
- *The action:* What classroom instructional method or approach are you changing or modifying for part or all of your subject group?
- *The outcome measure:* How or in what manner is the action going to be assessed?
- *A control group:* Who are you comparing your subject group to?

Not every inquiry will have all four components. For example, perhaps you are teaching a new course and you want to study the effectiveness of different assessment measures—such as in-class essay examinations versus take-home essay examinations—to evaluate student learning. In this inquiry, the subject group is your students, the action is their writing the different types of essays, and the outcome measure is their performance on the examination. There is no control group, since you have not taught the course before and are not teaching another section of it. This is not to say that this isn't a good inquiry project—studying assessment approaches is always well worth doing. But it will be more difficult to generalize the inquiry results. In fact, creating a control group can be problematic in classroom inquiry—in addition to the administrative difficulties of grading two different sets of assignments, there is also the ethical question that arises from not using what you believe to be the most effective teaching method for all students. Although it does not allow for an exact comparison, a possible solution is to compare student performance in the current term (which uses a new technique or approach) to that from a previous term (which was taught using a different technique or approach).

To get started, write a brief statement that casts the issue or problem you have identified as a question that you want to answer through your classroom inquiry. Your hypothesis should be concrete and clear, specifying the observable changes or outcomes that will allow objective evaluation of the results. Are there one or more alternative or additional questions that you might consider? Which question(s) will be most useful for improving student learning? Can your hypothesis be divided into smaller subquestions that you can address individually? Exhibit 1.8 shares the range of inquiry issues that are highlighted in the subsequent examples of the book. We will offer detailed commentary about each as we discuss them.

Exhibit 1.8
Range of Inquiry Examples in the Book

- Examining the impact of student assignments on student learning (Chapter 2)
- Evaluating students' ability to think critically and independently (Chapter 3)
- Employing different assessment strategies to gauge student learning and comprehension (Chapter 4)
- Assessing the impact of writing assignments in mathematics (Chapter 5)
- Assessing the impact of supplementary course materials on students' attitudes toward race (Chapter 6)
- Analyzing the impact of team size and composition for a service-learning project (Chapter 7)
- Using peer critique to improve examination performance (Chapter 8)
- Assessing the impact of Internet-based testing practices on student learning and attitudes (Chapter 9)
- Measuring the effectiveness of brainstorming methods (Chapter 10)

INQUIRY STEP 4
Developing an Investigative Plan

Once you have defined your inquiry hypothesis, you are ready to develop a plan for investigating it. This step is often the most difficult for teachers to conceptualize. To begin, you need to picture the type and range of classroom and student data that measures your inquiry hypothesis. *What, specifically, do you intend to do as you teach your course (e.g., introduce or modify specific teaching methods, revise course materials or assignments, collect examples of different types of student work) that will enable you to examine the issue you have identified? How will you collect the data that you need to answer your hypothesis?*

For many teachers, simply collecting and analyzing classroom data in a systematic way can yield very useful information about students' learning. You may find even more interesting and informative results if you develop an investigative plan that collects a broad range of qualitative and quantitative data. As the inquiry examples in the subsequent chapters illustrate, there are numerous ways to collect data to provide you with useful and empowering information about your students and your teaching. Traditional assessment strategies—graded student performance, student surveys, student teaching evaluations—have an important place in classroom inquiry. You might also want to move beyond focusing only on the student perspective by incorporating individuals or groups external to your course who can assist in your inquiry. Exhibit 1.9 provides some examples of nontraditional strategies for collecting data on a classroom inquiry question. Be careful in this, for trying to use too many different data sources might overwhelm you and your students. In general, keeping your investigative plan (and the resulting data collection requirements) focused and simple is usually best.

EXHIBIT 1.9
Some Nontraditional Strategies for Assessment

Strategy	Approach
Student commentary	Collect student thoughts and opinions via surveys, interviews, journals, or reflective statements on their own learning.
Classroom observations	Have a colleague observe your course (e.g., watching students interact in a small group discussion, observing a large class discussion, recording student participation).
Frequencies	Count frequency of events (e.g., percentage of class to get a wrong answer to a multiple-choice examination question, frequency of students to turn in homework late).

Counts	Tally number of students (e.g., classroom participation, students accessing review material stored on a web site, visits to your office).
External evaluators	Ask individuals external to your class (e.g., colleagues, alumni, industry partners) to assess your students' work and make a judgment of its quality.
Professional examinations	Link students' performance of your course topics to their success on professional examinations (e.g., nursing, engineering, teacher certification).
External recognition	Measure student success in using/applying work from your course in seeking external recognition (e.g., making a presentation at a school event or conference, winning a school or disciplinary award, publishing their work).
Student focus group	Ask a colleague to select a subset of your students and run a focus group in which they offer their perspectives on and opinions about their learning. The students might be asked: How do you prepare for (name the task)? What did the task ask you to do? What was helpful in undertaking it? What did you find difficult? Was it helpful to your learning? What would you improve?

In developing your investigative plan, strategize approaches that will ease your collection of classroom data. Some common methods include requiring students to submit their work electronically, using an online message board that will document student discussions, or having students develop a course portfolio of their classroom work that they turn in at the end of the term. An advantage of integrating your collection methods into your classroom activities is that it will promote your students' awareness of their own learning.

Exhibit 1.10 provides detailed prompts to consider as you develop and write your investigative plan. You don't have to develop assessment methods from scratch. There are several publications to help teachers conceptualize techniques and approaches for assessing student learning that can be seamlessly incorporated into your daily teaching life. Some include:

- Angelo and Cross (1993), *Classroom Assessment Techniques: A Handbook for College Teachers*

- Cross and Steadman (1996), *Classroom Research: Implementing the Scholarship of Teaching*
- Walvoord and Anderson (1998), *Effective Grading: A Tool for Learning and Assessment*

Exhibit 1.10
Prompts for Defining Your Investigative Plan

Major Category	Potential Items to Highlight
Inquiry scope	What do you already know about the issue that will assist you in investigating it? What do you need to know further about the issue in order to address it? (For example, if your problem is motivating students to prepare outside of class time, what do you know about how they currently prepare for your class? Is it an issue of time? Experience? Ability?)
Variables	What are the dependent and independent variables related to your inquiry? Dependent variables are those that you as the teacher have influence over (e.g., amount of homework you assign). Independent variables are those that you are seeking to measure (e.g., average examination score).
Classroom evidence	What classroom evidence or (qualitative and quantitative) data would help you to understand and/or address the issue more fully? Can your hypothesis be answered or proven with specific, observable phenomena from the classroom? If so, what phenomena might that be? How might you go about collecting this data or observing the phenomena that you need to further your investigation?
Other data sources	What other resources or avenues might provide you with useful information for studying or addressing this issue (e.g., student surveys, secondary reading of pedagogical literature, interviews with colleagues)?
Data collection strategy	How do you envision sampling (e.g., random, voluntary)? What will be the duration of data collection and the time interval (e.g., daily, weekly, once a term)? What is your sample size? Why do you feel this particular sampling will

	provide you with the data you need to explore your hypothesis?
Inquiry assumptions	What assumptions have you made about the nature of the issue or question you are investigating, about the conditions under which the issue occurs, about your methods and measurements, or about the relationship of this study to other persons and situations (e.g., your classroom presentation style will be similar to previous offerings of the course; your student population generally remains the same across repeated course offerings)? Are there assumptions that you can "test" via your data collection? How might you go about doing so?
Potential difficulties	What difficulties do you anticipate in studying this issue?

INQUIRY STEP 5
Relating Your Inquiry to What Has Been Done Before

At this point in the development of your classroom inquiry, it might be helpful to explore what types of investigations others have done that relate to your inquiry question. As we often tell our students, research doesn't take place in a vacuum. It builds on and contributes to existing conversations within a field or community. We began this chapter by saying that we did not want you to become an educational researcher, and that is still true. This inquiry step is optional, and we mention it for those readers who might want to publish or share their inquiry with external audiences and thus need to link their work to the work of others. Even if you intend to use your inquiry solely for formative improvement of your own teaching, though, you can learn from how other teachers have framed their inquiries. Such a process can validate your own thinking about a particular issue or perhaps raise new perspectives that you hadn't considered.

As you review and write about the work of others, you might highlight the critical points of current knowledge about your particular issue. It is helpful to summarize the results of existing studies and to describe who has addressed the topic, and when and where they carried out their studies. Questions to think about during your review of others' work might include:

- Can I improve upon their inquiry?
- How can I build on existing teaching conversations?
- How might my inquiry contribute to what's already been said?
- Does my work reframe or extend what others already know?
- Can I broaden the classroom situation in which the issue occurs?

Classroom inquiry work is made public in a variety of ways, from traditional print sources and conference proceedings to web pages and listservs. Exhibit 1.11 lists some places where you might find discussions that relate to your own inquiry.

EXHIBIT 1.11
General Resources for Exploring Others' Work on Your Inquiry Question

- Discipline-specific teaching journals
- Discipline-specific teaching conference proceedings
- Journals focused on the scholarship of teaching and learning
- National organizations that focus on the scholarship of teaching (e.g., the Carnegie Academy for the Advancement of Teaching, International Society for the Scholarship of Teaching and Learning)
- National organizations that focus on teaching (e.g., Professional and Organizational Development [POD] Network in Higher Education)
- Teaching papers written by faculty at your school (possibly available on a department web site or from your school's teaching and learning center)
- Books (in your school's library or available from your school's teaching and learning center)
- Discussions with the staff of your school's teaching and learning center
- Discussions with colleagues

One benefit from reviewing previous classroom inquiry work is that you will see how others have developed, measured, and presented similar inquiry issues. Pay attention to how authors have explained their variables, because how variables are measured can lead to the testing of very different hypotheses. As you engage in this work, you may notice differences between what you intend to do and what has been done. Some of those differences may actually lead you to go back and change your inquiry plans. But other differences are what make your classroom inquiry unique or different. Those differences may be small, such as placing students on teams based on an assessment of their abilities versus random assignment, or they may be more global, such as using a different strategy for data collection. But large or small, these variations contribute to the relevant teaching conversations.

INQUIRY STEP 6
Seeking Institutional Approval and Student Consent

Your reasons for conducting classroom inquiry—whether using it for your own growth as a teacher, including it as part of a department assessment, presenting the results at a conference, or writing a scholarly publication—will determine whether you need to get institutional approval for your inquiry project. Every school has a different policy regarding the institutional review of "experiments" involving human subjects, but in general, if your inquiry is for your development as a teacher, no review is required. If you foresee sharing or publishing your work with a wider audience, though, you should seek approval from your school's institutional review board (IRB). At some schools, this group might also be referred to as the ethics committee or the human subjects review committee. Classroom inquiry projects often fall into what is termed the *exempt category* of IRB approval, making the process fairly straightforward and relatively quick. If you have written a well-defined hypothesis and a plan for investigating it, it is often merely a matter of taking these details and putting them into the IRB format for your school. The actual procedures vary between schools, though, and are highly dependent on your school's experience in processing classroom inquiry proposals.

Whether or not you seek IRB approval, it is a matter of ethical practice to inform your students about your classroom inquiry and to obtain their permission to use their classroom data and examples of their coursework. Indeed, many teachers find it is valuable to engage students directly in their inquiry process. Exhibit 1.12 is an example of a form that you can modify for your own use. It is best to distribute and collect the form at the beginning of the term. It sometimes is useful to have someone external to your course (e.g., colleague, student worker, graduate assistant) distribute, collect, and hold on to the forms until the end of the term to minimize the perception of bias against students who do not wish to participate. In our experience, students overwhelmingly give their approval and are excited that you are interested in improving your teaching and their learning. One word of caution: there is a chance of the

Hawthorne effect influencing your data. This term refers to your observing improvements due to the fact that students know their work is being studied or observed. We have not found this to be a significant problem—and we all welcome anything that enhances student learning!—but it is a factor to be aware of, and it highlights the need to have a well-defined investigative plan that collects a range of classroom data and student performance.

Exhibit 1.12

Example of Student Consent Form

INFORMED STUDENT CONSENT STATEMENT

Course title: _____

Teacher name: _____

Semester/year: _____

Your teacher is conducting an inquiry into his or her teaching. He or she is examining the effectiveness of his or her instructional strategies, comparing, and/or evaluating the effectiveness of instructional techniques, curricula, or classroom management methods. This form requests your consent to allow your *classroom performance data* (e.g., examination scores, project grades, attendance records) and *coursework* (e.g., examinations, quizzes, papers, drawings) to be included as part of your teacher's classroom inquiry. Examples of actual student work are often very useful to demonstrate how much and how deeply students are learning. The form also asks you to allow your teacher to use these data for possible publication or presentation.

Your participation in this inquiry is voluntary, and there is no compensation should you choose to participate. The inquiry will be conducted as part of the class practice and activities as defined in your course syllabus. Your participation is not expected to require any added out-of-class time. Unless otherwise specified, your name will be removed from all coursework examples and you will not be referred to by name in any published materials or in any presentations. Once the classroom inquiry is complete, all copies of your coursework and/or examples that were retained by your teacher will be treated in the same manner as he or she maintains student work and records from other courses.

To indicate your willingness to have your *classroom performance data* included, please check one of the following two choices:

_____   I allow my classroom performance data to be included in my
           teacher's classroom inquiry.

_____   I do not allow my classroom performance data to be included in my
           teacher's classroom inquiry.

To indicate your willingness to have your *coursework* included, please check one of the following two choices:

_____   I allow copies of my coursework to be included in my teacher's
           classroom inquiry.

_____   I do not allow copies of my coursework to be included in my
           teacher's classroom inquiry.

If you are willing to have your *coursework* included, check one of the following two choices:

_____   I decline to have my name remain on any coursework that is
           included.

_____   I want my name to remain on any coursework that is included.

Please specify any additional restrictions on the use of your classroom work:

_____

_____

By signing below you give your permission for work you produce for this course (and your classroom performance data) to be used with the restrictions and for the purposes indicated above. You understand that your grade is *not* connected in any way with your participation in this inquiry, and that your anonymity will be maintained unless you designate otherwise. Finally, you understand that you are free to decide *not* to participate in this study or to withdraw at any time without adversely affecting your relationship with your teacher or the university, and withdrawal will not result in any loss of benefits to which you are otherwise entitled.

Your name (please print): _____

Your permanent address: _____

Email: _____

Signature: _____

Date: _____

If you have questions or concerns, please discuss them with your teacher *(Name, Department, Phone Number, Email)*. Additionally, if you have any questions about your rights as a study participant that have not been answered or to report any concerns about this study, you may contact the school's Institutional Review Board *(Phone Number)*.

INQUIRY STEP 7

Teaching the Course

Your inquiry question has been defined, your investigative plan is in place, and now it is time to teach your course. Exhibit 1.13 provides a checklist of items you need to complete during the term. For your classroom inquiry to be successful, you must pay special attention to collecting the data you need to analyze your hypothesis. Under the time pressures of teaching, research, and service, collecting the needed data for later analysis can easily get set aside or forgotten. For this reason, it is important that you identify approaches for simplifying your collection of the classroom data when you develop your investigative plan.

EXHIBIT 1.13

Checklist of Items to Complete During the Term

- Discuss the classroom inquiry project with your students.
- Distribute, collect, and store completed student consent forms.
- Scan, make photocopies, or keep electronic copies of selected student work (assignments, projects, examinations).
- Make photographs, videos, or audio recordings of student projects or performances.
- Occasionally review the data you are collecting to ensure it is answering your inquiry question. If not, adjust your data collection strategy.
- If you are having a colleague observe your course, discuss your goals for the class session prior to the visit(s).
- If using external evaluators, develop structured approaches (e.g., rubrics) so that they can provide useful feedback.

INQUIRY STEP 8
Interpreting and Evaluating Your Findings

Once you have taught your course and collected your classroom data, it's time to move to interpreting and analyzing your findings. As you write up the results of your classroom inquiry, it is important to develop useful structures for presenting the range of results, whether qualitative or quantitative, formal or informal. Exhibit 1.14 summarizes common methods for documenting the results of your classroom inquiry.

Exhibit 1.14
Common Approaches for Documenting a Classroom Inquiry

Approach	Example
Graphics	Use a pie chart, bar chart, graph, figure, or scatter plot to present results.
Student examples	Include copies or excerpts of student work (e.g., projects, term papers, examinations) that demonstrate the learning you are trying to achieve.
Classroom documents	Include examples of your classroom documents (e.g., project description, examination, grading rubric).
Numerical summaries	Summarize results using descriptive statistics (e.g., average, variation) or statistical analysis.
Multimedia	Provide photographs of student work, video of classroom presentations or discussions, or audio of student performances.

A key in presenting your results is not to get bogged down in using technical jargon or in sharing an endless collection of statistical comparisons. Explain your results using the tools from your first course in statistics, not your last—that is, use nothing more complicated than well-chosen descriptive techniques. Remember that readers of your work may come from outside of your field, and you may need to explain concepts or results that are self-evident to those within your discipline but that are foreign to those outside of it. Remember, too, that most future readers of your work will believe that shorter is better. They will not want to read a description of your classroom inquiry that includes lengthy examples of student work.

For this reason, when you discuss the learning demonstrated by a student paper, it is better to extract and highlight a paragraph from the paper rather than to include the entire document. Similarly, a 20-minute audio clip from a student recital could be reduced to a shorter 30- to 60-second highlight. One final word of caution when writing up your results: Be careful not to make overgeneralizations or sweeping comments that are not supported by the data you have collected. Exhibit 1.15 offers some questions to consider as you begin to evaluate your data. Exhibit 1.16 lists some general categories and prompts for writing your inquiry results.

Exhibit 1.15

Questions to Consider When Evaluating Your Data

- Which examples from your students' work demonstrate or support your hypothesis? Which classroom examples raise questions or issues for further study?
- How can you showcase the impact of the changes you made in your teaching? (For example, did the range of distribution regarding student performance on a particular assignment improve? Can you represent this improvement via a graph or a pie chart in comparison with previous course offerings?)
- How might you represent these findings (e.g., reflective summaries on passages from student papers, a statistical summary of students' improved test scores)?

Exhibit 1.16

Issues to Reflect on When Discussing Your Inquiry Results

Topic	Potential Items to Highlight
Uncontrolled factors	Were there any uncontrolled factors influencing the data that you collected?
Problems	Were there any problems in your investigative plan? Was there an error in your design? Did your approach yield the information that you thought it would?
Conclusions	What does the data you have collected tell you about the issue you originally chose to investigate? Does the data indicate your initial hypothesis is supported? Or does the data suggest that your initial hypothesis might be incorrect?

Relationship to other studies	How do your data results relate to your previous experience in teaching? Do they lead you to draw conclusions similar to those of previous studies?
Further study	Do you see a new hypothesis emerging? Are there new issues or questions arising from the data that you hadn't considered or that help you to reframe the issue(s)?

INQUIRY STEP 9
Reflecting on the Inquiry Process

The concluding step in your classroom inquiry is to offer some reflective commentary on your inquiry project, your journey in exploring it, and its impact on your students and on your teaching. Exhibit 1.17 offers detailed prompts you might find useful for structuring a final reflection on your classroom inquiry effort.

EXHIBIT 1.17
Prompts for Self-Reflection on Your Classroom Inquiry

Theme	Potential Items to Highlight
Impact on you	How has studying this issue or question helped you in the teaching of your course? What is the most important thing you learned about your teaching?
Student learning	What is the most important thing you learned about your students? Did your investigation help you to better meet your students' learning needs? What does your data analysis tell you about how students are learning? Is there evidence that the changes you made have improved students' learning/performance? Does student learning/performance indicate that they have a better understanding or appreciation of the issue that you identified?
Future inquiry and development	Are there particular features of the course that you will redesign? What specific changes do you plan to make in how you teach or organize the course? How do you think these changes will improve student understanding?

Broader impact	Do you see a need for curricular, programmatic, or departmental changes based on your investigation? How do the findings from your inquiry contribute to your own professional development and/or to the scholarship of teaching within your field or discipline?

CHECKLIST FOR ASSESSING CLASSROOM INQUIRY

Your classroom inquiry work is complete, you have finished the analysis, and you have written up the results. Now you might be wondering whether and how you should make your work public. Some questions you might be considering include, "How will others view my work?" "Does my documentation discuss all the important aspects of my classroom inquiry?" Building on the work of Wandt (1981) and Glassick et al. (1997), Exhibit 1.18 presents a detailed checklist for assessing your classroom inquiry work. While there are possibly characteristics on the checklist that do not relate to your inquiry, we present such a detailed list to share the entire range of issues that can be evaluated. You can use it as a guide to envision how others will review your work or give it to a colleague and ask that he or she review your work to identify the strengths and weaknesses of your classroom inquiry.

EXHIBIT 1.18
Assessment Checklist for a Classroom Inquiry Project

Characteristic	Strongly Agree	Agree	Indifferent	Disagree	Strongly Disagree	Not Applicable
CLEAR GOALS AND OBJECTIVES						
1. The hypothesis is clearly stated.						
2. The hypothesis is an important question in need of an answer.						
3. Answering the hypothesis is realistic and achievable.						
4. The problem/issue defining the hypothesis is put into context.						

Characteristic	Strongly Agree	Agree	Indifferent	Disagree	Strongly Disagree	Not Applicable
ADEQUATE PREPARATION						
5. The teacher brings the necessary skills to the inquiry project.						
6. The teacher has the resources necessary to explore the hypothesis.						
7. Relationship of the issue or problem to previous research is made clear.						
8. There is an understanding of existing scholarship in the field.						
APPROPRIATE METHODS						
9. Investigative plan is described fully.						
10. Investigative plan is appropriate for exploring the hypothesis.						
11. Investigative plan is free of shortcomings.						
12. Investigative plan is correctly modified in response to changing circumstances during the term.						
13. Data collection or sampling plan is defined.						
14. Method of sampling is appropriate.						
15. Data-gathering methods or procedures are appropriate for testing the hypothesis.						
16. Data-gathering methods or procedures are utilized correctly.						
17. Methods utilized in analyzing the data are correctly applied.						

Characteristic	Strongly Agree	Agree	Indifferent	Disagree	Strongly Disagree	Not Applicable
MEANINGFUL RESULTS						
18. Conclusions are clearly stated.						
19. Comparisons are appropriately connected.						
20. Conclusions are substantiated by the data presented.						
21. Generalizations are confined to the population from which the data was drawn.						
22. Alternative hypotheses or explanations of the data are ruled out.						
23. The results are interesting and useful to others.						
24. The results open additional areas for further exploration.						
CRITICAL REFLECTION						
25. The teacher critically evaluates his or her own work.						
26. The teacher brings an appropriate breadth of evidence to his or her critique.						
CLEAR COMMUNICATION						
27. Assumptions are clearly stated.						
28. Limitations are defined.						
29. Writing is clear, logical, and organized						
30. Work is written with clarity and without error.						

WHAT'S NEXT

Students often say that they can't fully understand a concept until they can see an example. We teachers are not unlike our students, so Chapters 2 through 10 present examples of classroom inquiries written by faculty from a range of academic disciplines. Our goal in showcasing actual examples is to provide you with practical and useful models to help you as you explore your own teaching. For each example, we comment on the teacher's approaches, methods, and findings. These comments highlight the successful aspects of their inquiry and evaluate the methodological choices that each teacher made in his or her inquiry project. In addition, we offer constructive suggestions for how the approach and documentation could be improved or done differently. These comments are intended to help you visualize how your own inquiry work will be received by others. The chapter examples are increasingly complex, with the first being a simple inquiry and the last being an example of scholarly teaching. Chapter 11 concludes with useful suggestions for getting started, discusses helpful external resources (national organizations, web sites, journals), links classroom inquiry to the larger conversations on the scholarship of teaching and learning, and addresses the different models you can use to disseminate your classroom inquiry work. We hope you find this book useful in facilitating your own journey into becoming a scholarly teacher.

CHAPTER TWO

THE BASIC STRUCTURE OF CLASSROOM INQUIRY

Following a structured inquiry process for analyzing my students' learning has transformed the way I develop course objectives, assignments, activities, and methods for assessing student work. The inquiry process keeps me intellectually engaged in constant refinement of my course.

—Dana Fritz

Inquiry overview: Dana evaluates the change to student learning that resulted from replacing two in-class studio drawing projects with out-of-class exercises in which students collect images that demonstrate fundamental course concepts in her first-year art course.

Highlights: This classroom inquiry focuses specifically on the impact of changing the type of work assigned to students. Because it uses only one method of data collection, this example presents a simple and straightforward approach for classroom inquiry. To answer her hypothesis about the effect of the new assignments, Dana concentrates on her students' perceptions and self-evaluations of their own learning. Dana's example is valuable particularly because she devotes the first section of her inquiry to providing a detailed explanation for her approach to teaching this class and the learning goals she sets for her students.

Course activities used to measure inquiry question: Homework/assignment; survey of student opinions.

Inquiry presentation includes: Self-reflection; student commentary; data table; copy of homework assignment; copy of student survey; excerpts from course syllabus.

ABOUT THE COURSE

My inquiry focuses on my perceptual drawing course—one of the four components in the Visual Literacy curriculum. Exhibit 2.1 shows my course details. Teaching a beginning-level perceptual drawing course gives me the opportunity to teach much more than just draftsmanship. It provides a forum for introducing new ways of seeing, thinking, and expressing that are essential in the development of an artist or designer.

EXHIBIT 2.1

Details of Dana's Course

Discipline	Art and Design (Visual Literacy Program)
Course	Perceptual Drawing
Course Level	First-year
Number of Students	29 (two sections of the course)
Type of Course	Targeted for majors in studio art, architecture, interior design, graphic design, and textiles
Meeting Time	Two 3-hour studio sessions per week, plus dedicated time for studio work

---

Since true drawing from observation depends more on seeing and perception than on manual dexterity with tools, I begin by helping my students to use their eyes in a new way. In her influential book, *The New Drawing on the Right Side of the Brain* (1999), Betty Edwards describes the "right brain shift" as a tool for learning to perceive a subject for drawing. When a student of drawing employs the right brain rather than the left, he or she moves away from naming and analysis into the nonverbal and the intuitive realm. In other words, when students stop drawing what they think they know, they start drawing what they really see. This different way of using the eyes is not only essential in perceptual drawing, it is useful in gaining a more complete awareness of the visual world. The process of perceptual drawing teaches one to observe, distinguish, and relate skills that can be expanded beyond the studio. This right-brained way of seeing coupled with a left-brain analysis of form and meaning leads to "Visual Literacy." Exhibit 2.2 lists my specific course objectives.

EXHIBIT 2.2
Dana's Course Objectives

1. To develop and utilize a design/drawing vocabulary
2. To understand the difference between the modes of naming and seeing
3. To develop strategies for evaluating your work and the work of others
4. To investigate work by artists and designers
5. To develop and implement compositional strategies for design and drawing
6. To utilize a viewfinder as a compositional aid
7. To competently represent three-dimensional objects and spaces on paper from observation
8. To develop a disciplined and reflective drawing and writing practice
9. To learn and apply a variety of techniques for seeing and drawing
10. To explore a variety of drawing materials

COMMENTARY 2.1

Dana's discussion of her course objectives offers a useful window into the changes she will make to her course and provides a broader context for understanding her inquiry. The process of outlining and linking course objectives in and of itself can often be pedagogically useful, and Dana could go even further in considering the relationships between her objectives. For instance, she might consider whether Objective 6 (to utilize a viewfinder as a compositional aid) is actually a subset of Objective 9 (to learn and apply a variety of techniques for seeing and drawing). In planning your own inquiry, connecting learning goals can help you identify which objectives are central to your course and how larger objectives can be divided into smaller and more specific (and measurable) components.

DEVELOPMENT OF THE INQUIRY

Visual Literacy suggests that we teach students to "read what they see." However, I believe that a real fluency in this area includes verbal articulation and critical thinking skills that complement the visual components of the course. These skills converge in my classroom during critiques and discussions of both student projects and historical and contemporary visual artifacts where students incorporate new art and design terms into their vocabulary. Active participation is required in my course because I believe that each student brings unique experiences and perspectives that, when shared, can be useful and even inspiring to others. Skills in description, interpretation, and evaluation are developed, tested, and honed in a supportive atmosphere.

Proficiency for drawing from observation is cultivated in a series of exercises that focus on the perception of edges, spaces, relationships, light, and shadow, which, when integrated, lead to perception of "the whole." These perceptions are what Betty Edwards (1999) identifies as the basic skills of drawing. These exercises, while focused on the eyes, also allow students to experiment with a variety of media and to learn the value of patience and persistence.

Throughout the course, students are required to keep a sketchbook. I encourage students to take visual notes in their sketchbooks during slide lectures to help them process and retain the images and information. Visual note taking as well as drawing from observation outside of class can accelerate a student's progress in drawing. Certain drawing assignments incorporate a sketchbook component, but students are free to put anything into it whether it relates to class or not. Students who seize this opportunity to weave their sketchbook into other aspects of their lives are likely to maintain a sketchbook long after my course is over.

Finally, I want to teach students to value the process as well as the products in their drawing explorations. Especially in the beginning, the product is secondary to, or simply a byproduct of, an active but sometimes elusive process. In the end, if they understand the process, they will always be able to make more drawings. While a portfolio is important, it is the process of seeing and the application of visual literacy that will be called on in all of a student's later pursuits in art and design.

COMMENTARY 2.2

Dana's reflective commentary shares important details of her course and her learning outcomes. Your own inquiry should share similar details of what you expect of students and what processes you have in place for them to achieve these expectations.

PUTTING THE ISSUE INTO CONTEXT

For my course, I plan to:

- *Add a required weekly "outside research" assignment* (see Exhibit 2.3).
  Through the outside research assignments I hope to teach students
  to become more self-directed and active in their studio work; to
  supplement their textbook with color images; and to help them
  realize that the basic concepts we are learning in perceptual drawing are not limited to the classroom but are actually used by professional artists and designers all over the world and throughout
  history.
- *Drop two previous required studio projects.* I don't want students to be
  spread too thin and pulled from too many directions.
- *Change the class meeting structure.* I will reduce the number of formal classes from three per week to two per week to provide students a designated time for outside research (which cannot be done
  in the studio) as well as time to revise work for their portfolios. It
  should also emphasize the importance of independent work and
  keep me from unnecessarily hovering over the students, so they can
  make their own aesthetic and technical decisions.

COMMENTARY 2.3

Dana's outside research assignment, in which students must search
for specific types of visual images outside of class, connects most
directly to her learning Objectives 4 (to investigate work by artists
and designers) and 9 (to learn and apply a variety of techniques for
seeing and drawing). The associated discussion should also support
Objective 1 (to develop and utilize a design/drawing vocabulary).
Also, Dana's use of the phrase "outside research" in her inquiry
might be confusing since other disciplinary areas often use this term
to describe a research paper or a literature survey. When you write
you own inquiry, keep in mind that those who read it may come
from a wide variety of disciplines, and you may need to define or
modify your vocabulary to meet the needs of this varied audience.

Exhibit 2.3
Student Handout Describing Outside Research

Outside Research

Each week you will be assigned to conduct outside visual research that parallels your drawing explorations and that will help to hone your visual literacy. *This research will benefit you the most if you do it before you begin your homework on the same subject.* This active learning process can help you to see and understand that the concepts from the studio are used by artists and designers for visual problem solving nearly everywhere you look. The resulting increased awareness and understanding is part of what is meant by the term "visual literacy." (This term goes well beyond being the title of your academic program; indeed, it is something you will utilize throughout your career and life.) This work will *usually* be assigned on Wednesdays and due on Mondays. (Fridays are reserved for you to visit the library or look for relevant conditions out in the world.) Each week's visual research will include:

1. *Three* photocopied or printed examples of the assigned visual topic. These images can be:
   • Photocopies from books, magazines, or other printed matter
   • Actual examples of printed matter (e.g., an exhibition announcement)
   • Printouts from Internet images (a maximum of *one* from the Internet each week)
   • Prints of digital photographs you have taken
2. A written account of the image's source, author, etc., and how it fits into the current week's topic. This must be attached to the image.
3. During the course, there will be six outside research topics:
   • Positive/Negative, Figure/Ground
   • Line/Edge
   • Cross-contour/Volume
   • Regulating Line
   • Value/Light
   • Time
4. Outside research will be presented and discussed on the due date each week. If given your thoughtful attention, this activity should complement your drawing explorations and increase your awareness of art and design. You will be asked to comment on it for your graded portfolio reflection. Keep your outside research all in one place (either in your

sketchbook or in your folder). If you feel that you already have a good understanding of the topic in relation to what is due for homework, take this opportunity to *expand* your understanding of the topic in new and unexpected ways.

INQUIRY HYPOTHESIS

My hypothesis is: *The conversion of some studio projects to outside research will significantly benefit my students' learning.* I will seek to answer several subquestions as I explore this hypothesis:

- Will students develop a habit of conducting outside research after my course?
- Will students value their outside research as a supplement to the textbook?
- Will the outside research teach students to look differently at their surroundings as they become more visually literate?

INVESTIGATIVE PLAN

To measure the impact of outside research on my course, I will use two approaches. First, as part of the regular classroom reflections that students turn in twice during the course, I will collect student comments on the impact of outside research. Second, at the end of the term, I will have students complete an anonymous survey asking directed questions about the outside research.

COMMENTARY 2.4

In defining her investigative plan, Dana focuses her inquiry on the impact of outside research on students' perceptions of their learning in her class. Her project is a good example of an inquiry that does not include a control group, as we discussed in Chapter 1. If she had wanted to include a control group, she could have treated her two course sections differently: one that completed the new outside research assignments, and the other that completed the removed studio projects. An alternative would be to compare student performance in the current term to that from a previous term.

INTERPRETING AND EVALUATING FINDINGS

Exhibit 2.4 provides a sample of student reflective comments to the question: *How has outside research increased your "visual literacy"?* Of the 29 collected reflections, the ones that I highlight reveal the diversity of comments. All of the reflective responses were positive regarding the value of outside research in developing visual literacy. No responses were negative, but some were less enthusiastic.

Exhibit 2.4

Sample of Student Reflective Comments on Impact of the Outside Research

Student 1: "Most of my outside research I have taken from ads. I never paid as much attention to the amount of work that must go into advertising. Now, flipping through even clothes catalogs, I look at the setup and the way the photographer has chosen to portray a certain emotion or idea. It truly has made me more perceptive, I pay attention to things I never used to, because now they interest me and I have a better understanding of why they choose to make elements look a particular way."

Student 2: "The outside research helped with my homework. I would find pieces of art before I started my own project. It gave me an idea of the limits I had to work with and how to broaden my assignment. This was especially true when I was inspired by works of cross-contour/volume. When it came to value and light, the outside research just got me excited about that topic. When you see some of the amazing things that value and light can do with a piece of art or a building, you can't help but want to create something of your own. Many times it is not your own outside research that is interesting, because you found it and were probably somewhat familiar with it. Instead it is seeing other students' research, things that you never would have come up with concerning that topic."

Student 3: "I think that the outside research is one of the most interesting parts of this class. When we are able to share what we have found for a particular subject we are able to share how we all individually think about each subject. I think being able to share these ideas allows all to then look at our own pictures again and think about them in a new way. I think this is also a way for us to all stay in touch with the outside world."

COMMENTARY 2.5

While the actual examples of student responses are useful, it would be helpful if Dana were able to somehow "classify" the comments of her 29 students according to how they responded to the outside research. She could then share summary statistics of the category results to give an overview of how all the students perceived the activity. As you plan your own inquiry, you might consider how to convert qualitative data into quantitative data in order to detect and illustrate trends or larger issues.

The students' reflective writing responses are heartening, but I must keep in mind that they receive a grade for their reflection and they also know what I want to read. Either they truly value the outside research assignments or they are trying to please me. Even so, I was impressed with the variety of positive responses and the details each of them used to describe how the assignment has increased their visual literacy. I was pleasantly surprised to read the comments of Students 2 and 3 about the value of sharing their outside research in class.

COMMENTARY 2.6

Dana's concerns about whether her students' reflections are simply mirroring what she wants to hear are important to consider. This concern is especially relevant because she is relying solely on students' perceptions of their experience for her inquiry data. In the future, Dana could look to extend the dimensions of her data collection by:

- *Supplementing the student voice by adding her own professional evaluation of the quality of her students' outside research.* This evaluation could be made by assigning formal grades or using other more informal ratings (for instance using high pass, pass, low pass) to differentiate among students work and/or to evaluate a student's improvement over the course of the semester, or by adding her own commentary describing student achievement on an assignment.
- *Comparing student achievement on the studio projects to their grades on the corresponding outside research assignments.*

> Either or both of these approaches would help alleviate Dana's concerns about student bias as well as further document the impact of the effectiveness of outside research on her students' learning.

During the final week of the term, students were given an anonymous survey. The survey sought a more objective and accurate reading of how students felt about the outside research requirement. The survey responses were anonymous and were collected by an assistant. The students' participation was voluntary and did not involve a grade. Not all students were present at the time of the survey so I had only 25 responses (in comparison to the 29 written reflections). The survey responses, shown in Exhibit 2.5, match the reflective writing comments and support my perception that the outside research assignment was indeed a valuable addition to my course. All of the surveyed students indicated that their outside research was helpful in increasing their understanding of the drawing exercises and helpful in expanding their knowledge of how artists and designers use similar concepts. Most of the students surveyed indicated that outside research is likely to become a regular part of their studio practice and that outside research has changed the way they look at the world.

Exhibit 2.5
Student Survey Responses

Question	Very Helpful	Somewhat Helpful	Not Helpful
Outside research was _____ in increasing my understanding of the drawing exercises.	48.0%	52.0%	0.0%
Outside research was _____ in expanding my knowledge of how artists and designers use similar concepts.	72.0%	28.0%	0.0%
Outside research is _____ to become a regular part of my studio practice.	32.0%	48.0%	24.0%

Question	Definitely	Partially	Not
Outside research has _____ changed the way I look at the world.	60.0%	36.0%	4.0%

COMMENTARY 2.7

If you use student surveys in your own inquiry project, you must consider how to balance the need for anonymity—so that students feel free to criticize—with the need for accountability—so that students take the assignment seriously. One possibility would be to make the reflection anonymous and give students in-class time to write it. Alternatively, if the reflections are not anonymous, an assistant could collect and hold the reflections until after the final grades are turned in. In Dana's case, even though the comments were anonymous, to ensure no bias, she had an assistant collect and hold them. The results of Dana's survey might be more informative if she had used a 5-point Likert scale (e.g., strongly disagree, disagree, neither agree or disagree, agree, strongly agree) for measuring a larger range of students' perceptions.

FINAL REFLECTION

Did I prove my hypothesis that *the conversion of some studio projects to outside research would significantly benefit my students' learning?* Yes, my students' outside research and the related discussions resulted in an impact on their learning. The loss of two studio projects is more than offset by the gain in "visual literacy." I can also address the subquestions that I posed:

- *Will students develop a habit of conducting outside research after my course?* Most of them will. Eighty percent of the surveyed students indicated that outside research is likely to become a regular part of their studio practice.
- *Will students value outside research as a supplement to the textbook?* Yes, 100% of the surveyed students indicated that outside research was helpful in increasing their understanding of the drawing exercises.

• *Will the outside research teach students to look differently at their surroundings as they become more visually literate?* Yes, 96% of my students indicated that outside research has changed the way they look at the world.

COMMENTARY 2.8

Dana's subquestions raise an important issue about learning outcomes because they concern the future behavior of her students. Dana's approach—asking students about their intentions for the future—is certainly valid. As teachers we all hope that our students will internalize and apply what we have taught them. One way to test if students have followed through on their intentions would be to interview or conduct a survey at a later time. This form of data collection would be very difficult for most courses, but in a tightly focused program such as the one in which Dana teaches, a delayed survey might be both feasible and valuable for those teaching subsequent courses in a sequence. In addition, similar questions could be incorporated into an exit survey given to graduating seniors, a common feature in many departments and programs. In this way, a classroom inquiry project could serve as a foundation for a department/program seeking to measure student learning for accreditation or review.

I will continue to include the outside research assignments in my perceptual drawing course because of its value as demonstrated by both the students' reflective writings and the survey results. Looking ahead, I next want to explore using a web-based academic portal (e.g., Blackboard) more fully in my course. I can envision introducing students to the outside research assignments using examples that are archived on Blackboard. I will then invite students to post some of their examples on the site's discussion board. Posting outside research images on the discussion board will provide students with access to far more examples than just using individual sketchbooks.

COMMENTARY 2.9

Dana's inquiry has led her to think about how to integrate her new assignment more fully into her course. Posting examples of student work to a web-based academic portal will broaden students' exposure to concepts she is teaching and will generate more classroom discussion. In this way, her inquiry is leading to pedagogical improvements in how her future courses will be structured. If she wished, Dana could take future inquiries into her class in a number of different directions. For instance, she could:

- Measure the quality of the student discussions about their outside research
- Evaluate the quality of the images that the students obtain
- Test the impact of the outside research on students' abilities to see, think, and express themselves
- Examine whether the amount of student learning differs among the six outside research projects

POSTSCRIPT

In the subsequent semesters, Dana has indeed developed the web-based academic portal so that her students can post and share their outside research (which she now calls "visual research"). She has students discuss their posts in small "critical peer" groups and then present the best of each group's submissions to the class. To focus the group discussions, she has reduced from three to two the number of images each student collects. Additionally, since the images are now shared in a digital format, she enforces more strictly the limit of one "Internet search" image for each topic and suggests that students scan images they find and/or use a digital camera. Although she has had difficulty using a web-based interface not designed to facilitate and support digital images, Dana has been able to document the positive impact of the digital archive on her students.

CHAPTER THREE

INCORPORATING ADDITIONAL FORMS OF DATA COLLECTION

Critical thinking is a common course goal, and I always thought I sort of knew what it meant. When working on my inquiry, I started to think about specific outcomes that would show the level of critical thinking that takes place in my classroom. It was and continues to be a very powerful experience for both my students and me.

—FRAUKE HACHTMANN

INQUIRY OVERVIEW: Frauke's inquiry examines how her classroom methods and practices develop student skills for thinking critically and independently in her combined fourth-year and graduate-level Advertising Media Strategy course.

HIGHLIGHTS: Frauke's inquiry examines student learning in a capstone course for pre-professional majors. Using detailed comments collected from her students, her inquiry examines the value of a particular pedagogical strategy—student peer review. As you read Frauke's inquiry, you might consider what "critical and independent thinking" looks like in your course (and discipline) and how you could document students attaining these skills.

COURSE ACTIVITIES USED TO MEASURE INQUIRY QUESTION: Student peer critique and review; survey of student opinions; comparison of final grades to previous term.

INQUIRY PRESENTATION INCLUDES: Self-reflection; student commentary; bar chart; example of student work; excerpts from course syllabus.

ABOUT THE COURSE

I have taught my Advertising Media Strategy course seven times. The course provides students with a basic understanding of mass media in the United States and shows them how the media planning process is incorporated into advertising strategy. Planning, selection, and evaluation of all major advertising media are the focus of this course, as are the various decisions that arise in these processes. Class discussions focus on strategic approaches to solving different challenges in advertising media planning. After students learn to create a strategy for a client that connects with an audience, they practice buying media that reaches these audiences effectively and efficiently. Discussions, assignments, and in-class exercises are geared toward practicing specific parts contained in a media plan, resulting in a term project focused on writing an actual media plan. Exhibit 3.1 shares details of my course and Exhibit 3.2 lists specific outcomes students should be able to perform at the end of the term.

EXHIBIT 3.1

Details of Frauke's Course

Discipline	Advertising
Course	Advertising Media Strategy
Course Level	Combined fourth-year and graduate-level
Number of Students	35 (two sections of the course)
Type of Course	The fifth course in a sequence of six required for all undergraduate advertising majors
Meeting Time	Two 75-minute class sessions per week

EXHIBIT 3.2

Specific Outcomes for Students Completing Frauke's Course

1. Become familiar with the terminology used in advertising media.
2. Develop tools for critical examination and evaluation of media strategies in advertising: Use and interpret syndicated research data; cost-per-thousand and cost-per-point comparative analysis.
3. Become familiar with a variety of media strategies and tactics used in advertising.

4. Develop skills necessary to write and execute advertising media plans.
5. Understand and apply basic statistical methods and concepts.
6. Evaluate other students' work individually and as part of a team.
7. Be prepared for an entry-level media position or be equipped with the basic knowledge to work with a media planner.

COMMENTARY 3.1

Frauke's course can be characterized as pre-professional and focuses on developing real-world skills that students will use after they graduate. Frauke's list of student outcomes provides readers with a clear understanding of the skills and abilities that students will develop in her course.

DEVELOPMENT OF THE INQUIRY

I require my students to develop and write a marketing-driven media plan for a specific consumer product as a term project. In order to teach them how to defend their decision, students are required to write a brief rationale for each objective and strategy they are setting in their project. Because the media plan is a function of the overall advertising plan, which in turn is a function of marketing, being able to articulate their rationale is a key component of their learning.

Reviewing their rationale provides me with a way to assess whether students can see the bigger picture in a marketing context. While some students have excelled in writing a rationale that clearly showed their understanding, I have been somewhat disappointed with most students' writing. They either didn't provide a justification at all or offered answers directly from the book (with and without proper citations) or from my lectures without including their own original thoughts. While these answers weren't necessarily incorrect, they did not provide evidence as to whether a student really understood why he or she made a particular strategic decision. In other words, my students have been writing rationales that reflect *what* I wanted them to think, not *how* I wanted them to think.

COMMENTARY 3.2

Frauke makes an important observation that while her students' rationales may reflect what she wants them to think, they do not necessarily provide evidence that students have internalized processes for their decision-making. As Frauke develops her inquiry methodology, she will need to consider how she can collect data that will address this distinction. In her case, simply collecting students' rationales will not provide her with insight into *why* the students made the choices that they did. Other data, such as student reflections on their rationales, might yield more conclusive proof of *how* students are thinking about media planning in her class.

PUTTING THE ISSUE INTO CONTEXT

Many of my students are minoring in marketing and understand the basic principles, but they are not always able to apply new materials to the larger marketing context (i.e., see the big picture). One reason might be the fact that my course is based on numbers, not words. The course is quite different from the other advertising courses that we offer, and many new concepts are introduced that students haven't been exposed to before. Some students tend to get lost in all of these new concepts, terms, and definitions, and they are unable to relate them back to the marketing problem they are asked to solve.

I have taken several steps to help students. For their term project, students have to write a complete media plan—identifying goals, objectives, and creative strategies. The project is complex and requires students to work consistently over the final four weeks of the term. Students complete the project in sections, turning one section in each week for review. Logistically, given the limited time frame of the project, I cannot review all my students' work. For this reason, I have decided to use peer review (students commenting on their fellow students' or peers' work) so that every student can get feedback from other students on his or her work. The discussion board on our school's web-based academic portal (Blackboard) provides a useful tool to host these discussions. This strategy will help students get feedback on their work, and encourage them to articulate their questions and comments to each other.

COMMENTARY 3.3

Frauke's realistic assessment of the time constraints she faces in providing feedback has led her to adopt a classroom strategy that benefits students, not only by receiving feedback but also by having them provide it. This strategy also might give her a lens through which to see *how* students are making sense of the project goals. That is, as students give feedback to one another, their responses will demonstrate to Frauke how the class as a whole is able to understand and articulate the big picture of her project goals. Offering peer commentary can be challenging to students because they usually have no experience in doing it. Frauke does not say whether she explained to students how to review others' work (what to look for, how to comment on it) or provided examples of helpful reviews. If she did, it would be helpful to include these details in her inquiry.

INQUIRY HYPOTHESIS

The central research question I would like to answer with my classroom inquiry is: *Are students able to think critically and independently in my Advertising Media Strategy course?* I am particularly interested in assessing students' ability to see the big picture and in evaluating the effectiveness of student peer review to help them reach this goal. To answer this question, I want to address two subquestions:

- Do students understand how the tools of strategic media planning fit into the bigger picture of advertising and marketing?
- Is student peer review an effective strategy to help students succeed in their individual writing of the media plan?

COMMENTARY 3.4

Frauke has chosen to state her classroom inquiry as a question. The central question that she asks is very broad: What does it mean to think critically? What does it mean to think independently? To answer these questions, Frauke has identified two smaller questions. There are many other questions she could explore in attempting to answer her central question, but these two are the ones she has identified as important for helping validate the goals for her media plan project.

INVESTIGATIVE PLAN

Each week, students are required to write a draft of each of the three project sections (situation analysis; media objectives and strategies; and media analysis and recommendations) of their media plans and post them on the online discussion board along with the rationale they used for creating them. After posting their section of the media plan, each student has two days to read sections of at least three other students' work and provide critical feedback using techniques learned in class. In addition to student feedback, I also provide commentary, making sure that the suggestions made by other students are indeed appropriate. My data, collected during the four-week process of writing their media plans, included:

- My review of students' posted comments on the rationale for their media plan sections.
- My assessment and review of the peer review comments that students provide each other.
- A student survey to measure the students' perceptions of the degree of difficulty of the term project as well as how helpful they thought the peer evaluations were in their own learning process. The survey is based on Diamond's (1989) "Evaluation of an Assignment" survey and was administered after they turned in their completed project.

COMMENTARY 3.5

By using the online discussion board, Frauke is able to automatically maintain an archive of student discussions/comments that she can later use as a resource when extracting examples to analyze for her inquiry project. Integrating data collection technologies into one's daily teaching routine is an effective strategy for ensuring that your classroom inquiry does not add additional time or logistical burdens.

INTERPRETING AND EVALUATING FINDINGS

The first part of the media plan project (situation analysis) requires students to base their media decisions on facts and figures that they have researched. Several students did an excellent job of offering peer review commentary, demonstrating that they were able to think critically and independently. Many of these comments focused on the use of numeric data to support strategic decisions. One student wrote:

> One thing I noticed is that there is no geographic information in your paper. You may also want to add the actual dollar amounts to the marketing objectives section, in addition to the percentage goals.

Other comments pertained to the product life cycle and the need to include numbers to back up decisions:

> Talk about the locations of Payless and the product life cycle in there so that we (the advertisers) know that Payless is in a decline and so we can work with that.

Another student demonstrated the ability to see how media planning fits into the larger marketing realm by stating:

> I would add a little more about the fact that women are able to buy a variety of shoes and styles due to the lower prices. I'd also suggest including seasonal sales info/assumptions to help determine the best times to buy advertising space.

This student made a connection to the volume of shoes that needed to be sold in order to reach a marketing objective and pointed out that the media schedule should coincide with sales patterns.

In the second part of the project (media objectives and strategies), students must set specific media objectives and then devise marketing-driven strategies that will help them achieve these objectives. One of the objectives students need to set is a budget amount that is based on past advertising budgets. This task proved to be challenging for several students, but they were not afraid to ask their peers for help. Some peer review suggestions were as simple as recognizing the difference between a marketing objective (which usually relates directly to sales) and an advertising objective (which usually relates to communication). One student comment simply stated:

> You may just want to mention that "changing the habits of 37% of the target audience" is the advertising objective, not the marketing object.

This comment shows that the student understands the role of advertising in the marketing context.

Another advanced way to describe and work with a target audience is to define it in terms of usage levels. Not all students did this, but one group in particular discussed usage levels, which showed that they were thinking about how objectives can be reached by fine-tuning the target audience. One student stated:

> When you talk about changing the extremely light users to light or moderate users, how do you measure their usage level? One time you said an extremely light user visited the store once in three months, but later you said they would need to buy two pairs of shoes as a light/moderate user. You may need to clarify what classifies a moderate user.

Exhibit 3.3 is an excerpt from one student's explanation of the way she derived her budget—it clearly indicates that she was able to think independently. The only instruction I had given in class was that they should look at the client's past advertising budgets in order to predict what it may be for the next fiscal year.

Exhibit 3.3
Example of Student Explanation

Okay, here's how I got the budget for the campaign . . . and I'm not sure if I did it correctly, but I'll tell you anyway: In 2003, Payless Shoe Source spent $62 million on advertising. Over a ten-month period in 2004, $43.5 million was spent on advertising (www.payless.com). Based on these figures, the estimated budget for this campaign will be $43.95 million dollars. Okay . . . they spent $62 mil. in 2003. Per month, that is $5.17 mil. In 2004, they spent $43.5 mil. in TEN months . . . not the whole year . . . so that is $4.35 mil. per month. So to find the total they spent in 2004, I took $43.5 mil (ten months) and added $8.70 mil (two months) to get a total of $52.2 mil. Then, I took $52.2 mil. and divided it by $62 mil . . . doing that, you get 84.19% . . . and if you subtract 84.19% from 100%, you find that the budget, from 2003 to 2004 decreased by 15.81%. So, to calculate our budget, I took $52.2 mil. (the total from 2004) and multiplied it by 15.81% (assuming that the decrease in the amount spent on advertising would be constant) and got $8.25 mil, the amount that the budget would decrease. So then I subtracted $8.25 mil. from $52.2 mil. and got $43.95 mil., the amount I set as my budget.

Students often have difficulty grasping the "reach and frequency" objectives in a media plan. Here is an example of how one student successfully offers advice to another:

> Good work here—I have just a few suggestions. First, you didn't mention if you are emphasizing reach or frequency—it looks like they are both pretty high. There is a page in the MFP book as well as a chapter in the book which explains when you should emphasize reach and when to emphasize frequency. Also, when giving reasons for the different media choices, there are two figures in the book, which give reasons why the different [media] are beneficial—you might back your choices up with some examples from these.

The final major section of the media plan project (media analysis and recommendations) requires students to analyze and synthesize statistical data in order to make strategic media recommendations. This component has often been the most difficult portion of the media plan because there are no necessarily right or wrong answers. One student peer recognized that, although quantitative analysis is important, media planners also need to consider qualitative values when making strategic decisions:

> I would suggest explaining a little more about why you chose primetime for your television vehicle since its CPP [cost-per-point] is so high. . . . I think it's the right choice, just maybe mention a little more about it. You might also want to mention why you didn't choose the other two in that section as well.

Another student explained why two other students calculated different numbers, showing that she saw the bigger picture, by correctly interpreting a media planning tool which had been introduced early on in the term and which students now had to apply in their media projects:

> CPP can vary depending on which spot markets we use and how many spot markets we use. The cost becomes different, thus the CPP is different as well.

COMMENTARY 3.6

Frauke provides several qualitative examples of the way peer responses demonstrate her students' understanding of course concepts. Because her students' peer comments are discursive in nature, Frauke presents them as such in her inquiry, providing excerpts that pertain to each phase of the media project. One way she could present her data differently would be to categorize the comments in terms of what the students focus on. For instance, some of the peer comments use specific terms from advertising, such as "usage levels" and "reach and frequency," reflecting students' facility with the course content, while other excerpts focus on students' opinions regarding the value of peer commentary. Classifying or tallying these different types of comments might help Frauke gain a better sense of the distribution in the types of comments students are making. Frauke might also consider creating a rubric for evaluating the peer comments, so that the resulting grade distributions would give a quantifiable measure of student performance. Such a rubric would formalize her assessment of the online discussions and help her document improvement in her students' abilities. It would also give her students a better sense of what she expects from the peer comments. In future course offerings, she could use these examples as models for her students.

The student survey provided some interesting results. One of the survey questions asked students to state in their own words what they learned from the media plan project. Many of the answers pertained to the details they had to pay attention to when crafting the plan. Students realized that each piece is a part of the bigger puzzle:

> I really learned how it all worked together. It's interesting to see the media-buying process in detail.

Several students commented on the budget, which is an important aspect in marketing strategy, and one that they had not paid much attention to in other advertising courses leading up to this one. One student learned:

> How to effectively allocate a budget into a national plan; how to allocate GRPs to achieve maximum (optimal, effective) reach and frequency, and that $43.95 million isn't a lot.

Some students commented directly on the media plan as a piece of marketing strategy:

[I] learned media from a marketing aspect. [The] overall understanding of the process is important to know even if you are in a
different realm such as creative.

Yet another student learned:

How to set marketing, communications, and advertising goals and
how to use numbers in those goals.

This answer is one that I had been working toward for the last few offerings of the course, and it appears that I may have reached that goal (for
at least one student).

Surprisingly, my students were eager to offer peer review commentary to their classmates. For example, in response to a student who did-
n't understand how to work out the media budget, a peer wrote:

As far as budget goes, . . . I worked on it last week so I'll make a
little note sheet to show you how we came up with the figures.

Another student explained correctly why one of her peer's numbers
was off:

I think the reason why the numbers are off is because I used the
raw number for the CPM and it looks like maybe you used the
circulation number?

More then half (52%) of my students found the peer review process
"very helpful," with another 39% finding it "somewhat helpful." None of
the students thought that it was not helpful at all, and only 9% found it
not particularly helpful. One of the open-ended questions on the survey
asked students to comment on the peer review process as a learning tool
for this project. Most students commented positively on the peer review
process for two reasons: 1) it helped them catch mistakes that they would
otherwise have missed, and 2) it helped them stay on track with the
assignment. One student noted:

[The] peer review throughout the assignment was very helpful—
[it] allowed us to share ideas and thoughts and critique to improve.

Another student pointed out that:

It was great to have sections posted at different times, so we
weren't waiting until the last minute to complete the assignment.

This same student indicated that it would have been helpful to see other components of the media plan (implementation) in the peer review as well (". . . I would have liked a peer review of the flowchart, too").

Some students were uncomfortable commenting on other students' work because they did not know if they would give adequate feedback. One student said:

> I don't like commenting on other people's work when I'm not even sure about my own.

Therefore, it is important for me to continually monitor students' feedback and point out any potential problems or errors immediately without intimidating the student. Another student thought that the peer review process was a waste of time and that:

> Time could have been better spent working on [the] actual media plan.

COMMENTARY 3.7

The frustration expressed in these final two comments might be due in part to students' anxiety about how to critique their peers' work rather than a rejection of using peer review as a whole. This anxiety might be alleviated by giving the students guidelines for making comments and examples of constructive approaches and by formulating rubrics for evaluating student comments that are then shared with the students. Furthermore, Frauke might use this evidence to develop and articulate a stronger rationale for using peer review for this particular project. Indeed, she might connect the use of peer review to the professional expectations of the advertising workplace, where teamwork and peer review are common practices.

Overall, did I answer my central question: *Are students able to think critically and independently in the Advertising Media Strategy course?* The peer review comments that students gave their classmates revealed that the majority of them were able to think critically by providing constructive criticism of their peers' work. In addition, the student survey results indicate that students are aware that media strategy is a component of advertising, which in turn represents a component in the marketing mix.

It can be concluded that the majority of students who have taken this course are indeed able to think critically and independently.

Implementing the peer review component into the media plan project has helped my students achieve this goal. Exhibit 3.4 shows the grade distribution for this project from this term as compared to the previous term, in which there was no peer review component. As can be seen, the number of A's or A–'s increased this term in comparison to the previous term. In addition, fewer projects scored below average (C or lower) compared to the previous term, with the exception of media plans that completely failed. It should be noted that all three media plans that received an F resulted from students who did not turn in the final media plan project.

EXHIBIT 3.4

Comparison of Grades for the Media Plan Project

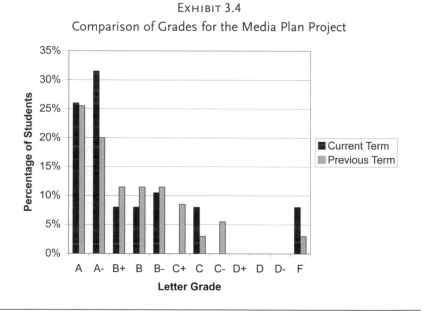

COMMENTARY 3.8

Frauke assesses the peer review component of her course by using the students' perceptions of their own learning as well as through a comparison of this term's project grades with those from a previous course offering. These two measures of student learning complement each other to give a more balanced view of student learning. In both cases, there were "outliers"—students who disliked the peer review process or who did not do well on their projects—however, the majority of students not only felt that they had learned more but also turned in projects that demonstrated a higher level of learning. Frauke's inquiry has given her solid evidence that answers her inquiry question with a strong "yes"—but as her final reflections will show, that is not the end of her inquiry process.

FINAL REFLECTION

Overall, the investigation helped me to improve the outcome of student learning on a crucial component in this course. Students appreciated the feedback of their peers, while they also recognized that everyone on the team has to participate in order for the peer responses to work.

The data show several areas for improvement. While the peer review process seems to be an effective tool in helping students succeed, it also adds to their workload. I had asked them to comment on three fellow students' sections each week, which turned out to be too much. I will reduce this amount in the future.

I noticed that some groups had much better discussions than others. Much of it depended on the students composing each group. Some of the groups included a graduate student, whose presence almost always added to the depth of the discussion. Next time, I will ensure that each group includes at least one graduate student.

The online student comments became less frequent and less thorough toward the end of the four-week project. Perhaps toward the end of the project (which is also the end of the term) students may have been too busy with other courses to continue to comment with the same frequency. Also, some students were unable to keep up with the suggested timeline, in which case they were not able to post their sections on time and then give and receive feedback. I will have students start working on the project earlier next term, which will also allow students time to revise their plans.

Another suggestion my students have made is to allocate some of the final grade to the quality of feedback students were giving. I will incorporate this suggestion into next term's syllabus.

In terms of my own professional development, my classroom inquiry provided evidence for several "hunches" I have had in the past. For example, I always knew that students could write better media plans by the questions they were asking me. The answers to their questions were issues

I had covered in class, but because of their complexity, my lectures and class discussions were not enough to really make an impact. I found myself answering similar questions all the time, and I was trying to find a better way to communicate them to all students, not just a few who were interested in excelling in the course. The student peer review process is an efficient and effective way to help answer students' questions. In addition, it gives students another opportunity to show me that they truly understand a particular topic by commenting on and critiquing other students' work.

COMMENTARY 3.9

While Frauke has offered strong evidence that the peer review process fostered her students' critical thinking abilities, her inquiry has also indicated several ways to improve that process. As a result, she has created a list of items she will change the next time she teaches the course, each of which might be the subject of another inquiry project. Some of these items correspond to points we have raised in our own commentary, such as creating a grading rubric for peer comments so that they can contribute to the final grade. Other items, such as changing the timeline for the project, will lead in a new direction. In any case, Frauke's inquiry has moved her farther down the road of scholarly teaching.

POSTSCRIPT

In a later offering of her course, Frauke implemented many of her planned changes. She discussed definitions of "critical thinking" with her students before explaining the peer review process. Using student work from the previous term, she shared with her students examples of each of the main project sections to illustrate the various levels of critical thinking.

To better manage the students' workload, she required each student to comment on only one other student's draft. This change resulted in more consistent posting of comments, especially toward the end of the term. Finally, she emphasized the peer review process by including it in the grading rubric for the final media plan project. She allocated enough points to the review process that engaging in the review had a significant effect on the final grade. Based on the grading rubric, students who chose not to actively participate could lose up to a full letter grade for their project.

CHAPTER FOUR

USING CLASSROOM INQUIRY TO ANSWER MULTIPLE QUESTIONS

I am much more systematic in thinking about outcomes and trying to tie the course experience to them. I think students find my courses are better organized and have a more unified message.

—CAROLYN EDWARDS

INQUIRY OVERVIEW: Carolyn's inquiry focuses on evaluating her students' learning through the use of different assessment strategies in her first-year early childhood education course.

HIGHLIGHTS: Carolyn looks at two different but related questions in her inquiry and then uses a variety of assessment measures to provide the data to answer those questions. She talks about how she shares her inquiry results with others. The result is a complex and richly detailed discussion of her classroom. While Carolyn's course is at the introductory level, its content is specifically designed around developing student competencies for meeting state certification. Carolyn must consider how the course she teaches is influenced by outside stakeholders, such as professional organizations, accreditation boards, and state/national certification standards. Drawing on the expectations of these stakeholders helps Carolyn identify important issues to study through her classroom inquiry.

COURSE ACTIVITIES USED TO MEASURE INQUIRY QUESTION: In-class activity; minute paper; examination; pre- and post-assessment.

INQUIRY PRESENTATION INCLUDES: Self-reflection; student commentary; data table; example of student answers; copy of examination question; excerpts from course syllabus.

ABOUT THE COURSE

My classroom inquiry project explores my Introduction to Early Care and Education course. This is one of the foundational courses for the Inclusive Early Childhood Education (ECE) teacher preparation program. Exhibit 4.1 lists details about my course. It is a required course, without prerequisites, taken very early on by students in the Inclusive ECE program. The course provides an introduction to the field of early care and education and applied child development. Students learn different philosophical and educational approaches to working with young children with a range of abilities in a variety of settings. They have direct contact with parents of young children and hear their stories in a question-and-answer setting. Students are expected to become aware of and articulate five key concepts or themes: Family Centered, Inclusive, Culturally Sensitive, Developmentally Appropriate, and Professional. They are also expected to gain competencies at the introductory ("awareness") level in 13 competencies needed to obtain certification by the state.

EXHIBIT 4.1

Details of Carolyn's Course

Discipline	Family and Consumer Science
Course	Introduction to Early Care and Education
Course Level	First-year
Number of Students	50
Type of Course	Primarily for students specializing in Inclusive Early Childhood Education
Meeting Time	Two 75-minute class sessions per week

Over the years, I have done a good deal of focused thinking and discussion with policymakers, faculty from four- and two-year colleges, community practitioners, and parent stakeholders about the mission, philosophy, and pedagogies of the Inclusive ECE teacher preparation program and the outcomes that we hope for in our students (Exhibit 4.2). In planning and teaching my course, I reflected deeply on these overarching program goals. I considered how my course, an introductory course and gateway to the program, could set the stage for students to be successful, to gain confidence and self-identity as professionals, to understand and incorporate professional ethical values, and to become excited and motivated to participate in their subsequent courses and field experiences in a way that would enhance everyone's learning from one another.

Exhibit 4.2

Goals for Students Completing the Inclusive ECE Program

1. Should have a broad knowledge and skill base to use in educating and caring for young children aged birth to grade three, across the entire range of abilities and disabilities, in developmentally appropriate and culturally sensitive ways

2. Should be able to partner with families and function in a variety of settings, including the natural environments of home and neighborhood, inclusive primary classrooms, kindergartens, preschools, childcare, and early intervention and special education settings

3. Should become conscious professionals who can collaborate with colleagues, partner with parents in child- and family-focused ways, use innovative, Italian-derived strategies of observation and documentation to plan curriculum, and continue to grow professionally and personally as they encounter new problems and situations after leaving school

---

COMMENTARY 4.1

Carolyn's classroom inquiry explores the effectiveness of her course in teaching the basic concepts that future early childhood educators need to know. As she develops her inquiry (and the course), she must account for the needs and requirements of many different external audiences—other teachers, schools, parents, program goals, and a state-based certification examination. In developing your own inquiry, you too may be challenged to balance different "voices" telling you what to teach.

DEVELOPMENT OF THE INQUIRY

My classroom inquiry focuses on improving my teaching and the students' learning about two of the key course concepts: *Developmentally Appropriate Practice* (DAP) and *Cultural Sensitivity*. The goals for my inquiry are to improve student learning by giving them 1) better awareness of how DAP and cultural sensitivity relate to their future professional development and training; 2) better skills in defining, recognizing, and applying these concepts in the context of real-world situations and problems; and 3) more positive motivation to instantiate the principles behind these concepts (i.e., to teach in developmentally appropriate ways and seek cultural sensitivity in interactions with both adults and children).

I decided to focus on DAP after a preliminary review of the graded and ungraded student work gathered from a previous term in which I taught this course. In one of the final class meetings, I asked the students to write one or more sentences about each of the five concepts of the course—what ideas had stood out for them, and/or what class activities had helped them to learn about each one. The key concept that students had least to say about was DAP. Many students did comment positively on the guest speakers who had come to class on three occasions to describe their curriculum and teaching strategies, but more students mentioned them in the context of learning about the concept of professionalism than for the concept of DAP. While a great deal of the course content relates to the concept of DAP, that underlying organization evidently was not visible to the students. This caused concern, since DAP has to do with the crucial topic of curriculum planning. It is also important for broad reasons related to the current state and national policy contexts concerning teacher education and early childhood education. For example, in order to respond to federal mandates of the "No Child Left Behind Act" of 2001 and the "Good Start, Grow Smart Initiative" of 2002, our state's Department of Education has worked with administrators, teachers, college faculty, parents, and citizens to create a set of Early Learning Guidelines that lay out what children in the preschool years can be expected to know across all the domains, suggested adult teaching behaviors, and adaptations to include children with special needs. These guidelines, along with state kindergarten to grade three standards, can be understood as defining a teaching framework for our state's early childhood educators.

For the concept of Cultural Sensitivity, in contrast, students in my previous course described how enthusiastic and moved they had been by the two class sessions taught by my graduate assistant, Toni Hill-Menson, who was a partner in teaching the class. Toni was able to lecture authentically about issues of prejudice/racism and had extensive training and expertise in multicultural education. Even with this positive impact of the multicultural unit, I was motivated to evaluate the depth of their understanding, since my course is the gateway course to the Inclusive ECE program and sets the stage for students in terms of the values and skills that they will take forward to the rest of their studies in the teacher preparation sequence.

COMMENTARY 4.2

Carolyn's inquiry is based on the specific findings of a previous offering of the course. Her analysis of her previous class has led her to focus on one area where she knows student learning should be increased and on another where she wants to measure the depth of perceived student learning. Carolyn is not content to rely simply on students' perceptions of their learning; she seeks to document the learning.

PUTTING THE ISSUE INTO CONTEXT

For my classroom inquiry, my aim is to help students develop an intellectual and emotional awareness of what it means for an early childhood professional to be *culturally sensitive* and to use *developmentally appropriate practice* with young children (birth through grade three) and their families.

INQUIRY HYPOTHESIS

My classroom inquiry is broken into two main questions, one about DAP and one about Culturally Sensitive practice:

- *DAP question:* Can students move from a vague and global understanding of the concept of DAP to a more differentiated understanding that involves the idea that 1) developmentally appropriate teaching is coordinated with individual students' learning in three ways: *age* appropriateness, *individual* appropriateness, and *cultural/family* appropriateness, and 2) that DAP involves active learning experiences, varied instructional strategies, balance between teacher- and child-directed activities, integrated curriculum, and learning centers?
- *Cultural Sensitivity question:* Can students learn that multicultural education refers in a broad way to education that reaches beyond

differences about race and culture to include all kinds of human diversity, in order to respect the child, family, and community with appreciation of each person's unique history and context? Because everyone has a unique history and context, can students learn that multicultural education begins with the self and with knowledge about one's own cultural history and background?

COMMENTARY 4.3

Rather than posing her inquiry in terms of a hypothesis to prove or disprove, Carolyn chose to define her inquiry in terms of two major questions to explore. Carolyn's complete inquiry project (available at www.courseportfolio.org) actually explores five questions: three on DAP, one on cultural sensitivity, and one on the interaction between the two. For brevity, we highlight only two of her questions. The highlighted questions articulate the criteria that she will use to assess student understanding of the concepts. For instance, for DAP she outlines three domains of understanding that students will need to demonstrate in order to show what she terms *differentiated understanding* of the concept. One challenge Carolyn faces is to document the ways which students recognize and apply these principles of DAP and Cultural Sensitivity to particular contexts rather than them simply "parroting" what they think she wants to hear.

INVESTIGATIVE PLAN

To carry out my classroom inquiry, Toni and I developed a set of assessment techniques selected from *Classroom Assessment Techniques* by Angelo and Cross (1993). We implemented a series of in-class assessment activities during the mid-portion of the course where the concepts of DAP and Culturally Sensitive practice were reflected on by students. We termed this quick and instant feedback *immediate assessment*. We also used multiple-choice and essay questions on the second course examination to assess student learning. Because students responded to these questions after the classroom presentation/discussion and they had time to reflect on what they learned, we termed this feedback *delayed assessment*.

COMMENTARY 4.4

Carolyn's distinction between immediate and delayed assessment is one you might find helpful. Immediate assessment is particularly useful for indicating whether students have understood material you have just presented. It can usually be carried out quickly and informally, and it may or may not result in written documentation of student learning. Examples of immediate assessment include having students write a minute paper, having them raise their hands (or select an answer using a personal response system, or "clicker") in response to an issue or question, or having them discuss a topic or issue. Delayed assessment measures learning or growth after students have had time to reflect on or study the issue or course material. They are more formal, require more preparation from both teacher and students, and yield documented results. Common examples are examinations, term papers, or homework assignments.

INTERPRETING AND EVALUATING FINDINGS

To answer the DAP question, we used an immediate assessment strategy of having the students write a minute paper after each presentation by an external speaker. Students were asked to write about:

- What was new and interesting to you about the presentation today?
- How is this speaker's approach developmentally appropriate?
- What questions do you still have?

One advantage of repeating the use of a minute paper with each external speaker was that students began to anticipate it and internalized the prompts. In our analysis of the minute papers, it became apparent that most students picked up on one aspect (age, individual, or cultural/family), but not on all three. Exhibit 4.3 shares sample excerpts.

Exhibit 4.3

Excerpts of Comments From Students' Minute Papers

- "Respects that every child has the ability to learn and express the way they see the world" and "Children work at their own pace and the teachers can see their progress." (Teaching *coordinated* with children's learning)

- "Allows children to learn how to do things other children do at their age." (*Age* appropriate)
- "Works with the children's developmental delays." (*Individually* appropriate)
- "Understands the kids' need for love and sense of belonging." (*Cultural and social* context)

COMMENTARY 4.5

Carolyn's observation that students were anticipating and internalizing the prompts for the minute paper illustrates the ways that assessment can reinforce and cycle back into student learning. The repetition of the assessment helped prepare students to listen more closely to the speakers and connect their talks to course concepts. In developing a similar prompt for future course offerings, Carolyn might consider incorporating questions that focus on each aspect of DAP so that students are more conscious of these aspects as they engage with the speakers.

After our analysis, Toni and I realized that students were grasping portions of the idea of DAP, but not the whole concept; hence, their understanding of the concept was still vague and global. We then prepared a one-page handout for students that succinctly and explicitly laid out a definition of DAP; clarified the aspects of age, individual, and cultural appropriateness; and summarized ideas about active learning experiences, varied instructional strategies, balance between teacher- and child-directed activities, integrated curriculum, and learning centers. Students seemed to appreciate this handout and to find it useful.

COMMENTARY 4.6

Notice how Carolyn used the results of the immediate assessment to adjust and modify the course as it went along. As part of her inquiry, Carolyn did not include a copy of the developed DAP handout. Adding it to her classroom inquiry documentation would help readers to see what she expected students to learn. Overall, her use of a feedback cycle takes time and effort but is very effective for improving a course.

As a means of measuring a delayed assessment, we added several specific questions about DAP to the second examination for the course. One multiple-choice question (Exhibit 4.4) asked students to recognize the three aspects of DAP. This question was answered correctly (Answer c) by 90% of the students, suggesting they had retained the information from the handout and learned that gender appropriateness is not part of the basic definition of DAP.

Exhibit 4.4

First DAP Question From the Second Examination

Which one of these is *not* one of the three key dimensions of developmentally appropriate practice?

(a) Age appropriate
(b) Individually appropriate
(c) Gender appropriate
(d) Takes account of the child's cultural and social context

A second multiple-choice question (Exhibit 4.5) asked students to apply the idea of DAP by choosing which example of teaching represents the concept: This question was answered correctly by 88% (Answer a), again suggesting they had retained the relevant information and were even able to apply it as well.

Exhibit 4.5

Second DAP Question From the Second Examination

Which one of these teachers seems to be using developmentally appropriate practice?

(a) Mrs. Edwards uses a large-group meeting followed by small group and individual work.
(b) Mr. Snope has learning centers for math and literacy. He thinks these two subjects are so important that he has taken every other subject area out of his curriculum.
(c) Mrs. Carta never directly instructs children and lets them lead all their learning and play.
(d) Miss Girard tries not to find out anything about children's family and backgrounds because she is afraid that information will prejudice her.

In the same examination, students were given a choice to answer one of three short essay questions from a selection of alternatives. One of the choices (Exhibit 4.6) gave them the opportunity to use knowledge about DAP to reflect on their own experiences as a young learner and comment on which curriculum model might have best suited their needs. Of the 50 students in the course, 27 chose this essay question. We examined the first part of their answers, explaining why they thought their own early childhood education was or was not developmentally appropriate. In this way, we hoped to determine whether the students applied the various aspects of DAP, including age, individual, and cultural/family appropriateness.

EXHIBIT 4.6

First DAP Essay Question From the Second Examination

Think back to when you were a young child. What were your specific learning strengths and weaknesses?

1. Discuss how your own education was and was not developmentally appropriate for you (you will want to think about the characteristics of DAP in answering this).
2. Then say which *one* of these would have best met your developmental needs as a young child, and why: (a) Reggio Emilia approach; (b) High/Scope approach; (c) Montessori education.

Exhibit 4.7 summarizes a sample of the answers. In examining the first column of the exhibit, "What I needed as a young learner," it is clear that when focusing on what they remembered about themselves as young learners, the students clearly apply the concept of *individual* appropriateness. They describe how their own individual needs (for more challenge, or more support in a particular subject area, or more teaching oriented to visual learners, or more autonomy, etc.) were not met. They also address *age* appropriateness (e.g., saying they had too many worksheets and whole-group teaching, or nothing really interesting to do other than wander around and play with the same toys). However, they do not bring up issues of *cultural/family* appropriateness (e.g., no one says their gender, ethnicity, language, or economic status made them receive poorer treatment, or that they felt ridiculed or humiliated in some way because of their identity or attributes).

EXHIBIT 4.7

Sample of Student Responses to the First DAP Essay Question

What I Needed as a Young Learner	I Would Have Enjoyed
I needed more help to learn reading (e.g., visual tools).	Montessori
I needed more challenge, but would have liked key experiences, plan to review, chance to expand knowledge with teacher guidance.	High/Scope
I wanted more choice, plan to review, and key experiences.	High/Scope
I would have liked an integrated curriculum and art projects incorporated.	Reggio
I was mature, learned quickly, and was stuck in a room with some toys; Montessori too structured, High/Scope to plan to review, Reggio too many projects. I would have liked some activities from each, doing things on own.	Combination
I was shy, quiet, good in literacy, liked mixed age, attended small school.	none

COMMENTARY 4.7

It's interesting that students didn't bring up issues of cultural/family appropriateness. Perhaps her class population was so homogeneous (e.g., white, middle class, and female) that they found it difficult to view their experiences in terms of culture (because they were from the "norm"). Here is a place where it might have been useful for Carolyn to discuss the population demographics of her course as a way to better consider what her students need in order to truly understand the cultural domain of DAP. This might also highlight possible gaps that she could address in future course offerings.

Another essay choice on the second examination (Exhibit 4.8) invited students to apply the concept of DAP to the primary-aged learner, and then apply further by describing how a particular guest speaker's teaching was developmentally appropriate for K–1 learners. Of the 50 students, 8 chose this essay question. We examined their answers to determine whether the students recalled the various aspects of DAP, including age, individual, and cultural/family appropriateness, and used them in analyzing the guest teacher's work. Exhibit 4.9 briefly summarizes all of their answers in a way that makes it easy to see the general trends. The *age* and *individual* appropriate aspects of the two guest teachers' work was clearly evident to the students, as seen in the examples they discussed, but the *cultural/family* appropriate aspect was not visible.

Exhibit 4.8

Second DAP Essay Question From the Second Examination

Define the characteristics of *developmentally appropriate practice* in the primary classroom and apply them to the specific characteristics (physical, cognitive, social, moral) of 6–9-year-old children. Then describe why the teacher was developmentally appropriate in her teaching approach for *one* of these two: Teacher A or Teacher B.

Exhibit 4.9

Summary of Student Responses to the Second DAP Essay Question

Teacher	Age Appropriate	Individually Appropriate	Culture/ Family
Teacher A	Concrete/abstract	Work alone and in small groups	Mentioned, no example
Teacher A	Used praise, learning centers	Small and large groups	Mentioned, no example
Teacher B	Active learning, learning centers	Observe and follow up on individual needs; own pace	Mentioned, no example
Teacher A	Active learning, integrated curriculum, learning centers	Varied instructional activities, choice	Mentioned, no example

Teacher	Age Appropriate	Individually Appropriate	Culture/ Family
Teacher A	Active learning, teacher and child directed, integrated curriculum, learning centers	Varied curriculum, high expectations	Mentioned, no example
Teacher B	Recess, gym, active learning, small groups, class discussions	Choice time, individual work time, own pace	Mentioned, no example
Teacher B	Discussed curriculum areas: cognitive, physical, social, moral	Own pace without pushing, chance to excel	Not mentioned
Teacher A	Balance child and teacher-led, varied instructional practice, small and large group, active learning—hands-on, wants to be responsible, wants cooperation, autonomy, active learning, exploration, choice	Separate individuals, not miniature adults	Not mentioned

---

COMMENTARY 4.8

It's surprising that so few students chose to write the second essay question and that none of the eight chose to write on cultural/family aspects—perhaps this finding highlights the need to provide more focused engagement on these issues since students seem to be avoiding or ignoring them.

To introduce students to Cultural Sensitivity practices, Toni uses a course activity in which students are asked to identify their own cultural issues through exercises involving family photographs that they bring to class and by sharing the origin of their names. It appeared that students were getting the message. Students actively participated in small and large group discussions. They eagerly shared stories about themselves and their families, demonstrating insight about their own cultural backgrounds.

During the unit, students also did an ungraded class activity (an immediate assessment) in which they looked for and listed both explicit and implicit references to culture in the National Association for the Education of Young Children ethical guidelines. In the writing they turned in, all students provided clear evidence that they could critically analyze the guidelines using their own definitions of explicit and implicit cultural references. Most of them found several examples of each. The findings suggest that the students were beginning to demonstrate an understanding that multicultural education goes beyond surface teaching about "customs and artifacts from other cultures and nations" (sometimes called a "tourist curriculum" approach) and that it instead reaches to a deeper level of multiculturalism involving respect for every person's family, history, and unique characteristics.

COMMENTARY 4.9

As part of her inquiry documentation, it would be helpful if Carolyn had included examples of her students' writing evidence or some quantitative details (e.g., graphics, summary statistics) categorizing the range of student responses. Another approach would be to share the results from having a colleague observe and summarize the classroom interactions/discussions.

To more formally assess learning in the multicultural unit, Toni used an in-class assessment based on a pre-test, post-test design as students began and ended the two-day unit on Cultural Sensitivity. Exhibit 4.10 lists the two questions she asked. On the pre-test, only 66% of students correctly answered the first question and only 22% correctly answered the second. However, on the post-test (using the same questions), these percentages rose to 97% for the first question and 86% for the second, suggesting students had learned the basic concepts when immediately assessed. Additionally, on the post-test, she asked them to answer the question: *What did you learn during the multicultural unit?* Exhibit 4.11 shares some of the answers.

EXHIBIT 4.10

Cultural Sensitivity Questions Asked of Students

- Race and ethnicity are the primary focus of multicultural education. (True/False)
- Ethnographic interviewing requires extensive research and preparation on other cultures. (True/False)

EXHIBIT 4.11

Student Answers to the Post-Test Question

- "There are more aspects of multiculturalism than I ever thought. It brings light to the saying, 'No two people are alike.'"
- "I learned that it doesn't always have to do with race. It can be gender, physical aspects, etc."
- "There are many ways to have a diverse classroom and the importance of valuing every individual."
- "I learned different ways of incorporating multicultural education in the classroom. It's more than just Black History Month."
- "I learned some ways to include multicultural activities into daily activities in the classroom. I also learned ways to enhance my awareness and sensitivity."
- "We as teachers need to really get to know as many aspects of our students' worlds to better connect with them and embrace the diversity."
- "Every child has a different background, and we need to accommodate that."

COMMENTARY 4.10

While many faculty use a pre- and post-test to measure learning occurring over an entire term, Carolyn and Toni used this assessment method to measure the learning resulting from a specific unit of instruction. The true/false questions show that learning occurred, while the written question allowed students to express the way their thinking on the topic had changed. This combination of quantitative and qualitative questions provided Carolyn and Toni with multiple forms of feedback regarding their students' engagement with multicultural concepts.

In addition, as a follow-up and delayed assessment, we reassessed student knowledge on the second examination using two multiple-choice questions (Exhibit 4.12) to determine whether they understood multicultural education in a broad rather than narrow perspective. The first question was answered correctly (Answer e) by 98% of the students, suggesting that all students had learned the broadened definition of the term *multicultural awareness.* The second question was answered correctly (Answer b) by 80%, with the other 20% selecting a wrong choice (Answer a), suggesting that most students were able to apply the concept and see the variety of ways in which multicultural education can be infused throughout the curriculum (without eliminating birthdays and holidays, which is not really necessary to do).

EXHIBIT 4.12

Cultural Sensitivity Questions on the Second Examination

Question 1

Multicultural awareness is the appreciation for and understanding of people's _____.

(a) Cultures
(b) Socioeconomic status
(c) Gender
(d) Race
(e) All of the above

Question 2

Infusion of multicultural education processes into the early childhood curriculum is accomplished by 1) fostering cultural awareness; 2) promoting conflict resolution strategies; 3) teaching to children's learning styles; 4) eliminating celebration of birthdays; 5) eliminating celebration of holidays from the curriculum.

(a) 1 only
(b) 1, 2, and 3
(c) 1, 4, and 5
(d) All of the above

COMMENTARY 4.11

Through her inquiry, Carolyn was able to develop an understanding of her students' learning and progress. As was the case with the described pre- and post-tests, the combination of qualitative and quantitative approaches provided complementary measures of the depth of her students' understanding. Her results have raised important issues for her to consider regarding students' understanding of and familiarity with cultural sensitivity practices. They have revealed that students are not referring to cultural sensitivity in analyzing their own experiences and those of others. These results can be very useful in modifying course assignments and practices to ensure that students get this exposure.

FINAL REFLECTION

My classroom inquiry project proved very illuminating to Toni and me and will help improve our teaching of the course in the future. First, the inquiry demonstrated the utility of immediate in-class assessment strategies, such as the minute papers and pre- and post-tests, in making adjustments in teaching to clarify material, reinforce concepts, and affirm students. The trick that I need to remember is to analyze and interpret these products right away so that the findings can help steer my next steps in the classroom. I had not realized how informative it can be to use class activity papers as assessments and as a way to step up instruction for the students' immediate benefit. The adjustments suggested by these tools and our continuous analysis of the in-class assessments improved the course.

Once our analysis of the inquiry was complete, with my help Toni developed a poster of the results which was displayed at two research fairs the next semester at our school (available at http://digitalcommons.unl.edu/famconfacpub/27/). The poster stimulated good conversations, and Toni won the graduate student poster competition.

COMMENTARY 4.12

Carolyn's discussion of her results with her students demonstrates one important use for classroom inquiry. Sharing your inquiry work with your students often allows them to see the big picture of the learning you want them to achieve. The poster that Toni and Carolyn created for display at their school research fairs makes the inquiry publicly available to a wide audience—current students, future students, parents, colleagues, and administrators. Since Carolyn's course is viewed as foundational, this public display allows instructors of courses taught later in the early childhood education sequence to see what her students know in the five topic domains. This knowledge will allow them to connect to and build on what these students have already learned and experienced. In planning your inquiry project, envision some "public" avenues you might use to make your work visible. The fact that they won a research poster competition for this work is an added bonus—an affirmation that classroom inquiry is an important form of a scholarly activity at their school.

Completing my classroom inquiry project has suggested to me the following specific recommendations to improve the course:

- Introduce the concept of DAP via the handout we created prior to the guest speakers coming to class.
- After each guest speaker, again use minute papers to assess the immediate impact, and share with the students examples of good responses that highlight aspects of DAP and show their insight about the three curriculum models. This debriefing will both reinforce and affirm their emerging knowledge and share with them good role models they can emulate.
- In class, have students discuss their own early childhood experiences as a way to think about individual appropriateness.
- Use case studies to forefront the issues of cultural/family appropriateness.
- Continue to use essay questions on the second examination, as these seem to give students the best opportunity to demonstrate their knowledge about the concepts. Revise the essay questions on

the second exam to clarify what is desired for a complete answer.

- During the unit on Cultural Sensitivity, introduce an in-class activity where students are provided a variety of examples of activities that could be used with different age groups of children. Have students discuss those that are and those that are not developmentally appropriate and culturally sensitive, and why. Include examples that go across the range of good and bad teaching.

- Develop a poster of my classroom inquiry results to be displayed in the department. Also, discuss the results in future offerings of the course.

COMMENTARY 4.13

Carolyn was a successful teacher before she began her inquiry, but as a result of the detailed examination of her course, she has developed several ways in which she can further improve her teaching effectiveness. Her case illustrates how development as a scholarly teacher is a continuing journey.

POSTSCRIPT

In planning her next offering of this course, Carolyn is going to use even more immediate assessment strategies to guide the teaching of the class. Furthermore, she and her teaching assistant plan to present their poster at a national conference of early childhood educators to see how others react to their strategies and findings.

CHAPTER FIVE

OVERCOMING CHALLENGES WITH DATA COLLECTION

This inquiry has been most useful in two ways. First it forced me to assess a desired outcome in a systematic manner. Second, it provided a record that I can reflect on and build on the next time I teach a similar course.

—GORDON WOODWARD

INQUIRY OVERVIEW: Gordon wants to know whether having students complete a weekly essay homework assignment improves their ability to explain and discuss mathematical concepts in an accurate and coherent manner in his fourth-year and graduate-level course for present and future mathematics teachers.

HIGHLIGHTS: During his inquiry, Gordon encounters several challenges that many teachers commonly face, including difficulties in collecting student work and making useful comparisons about student performance on different course assignments. Gordon is interested in helping his students develop their writing as a learning tool that they might use in their own teaching. While he was unable to draw definite conclusions about the improvement of their writing skills, the process of developing his inquiry, collecting the data, and analyzing the issue generated strategies to improve the course design and refine his strategies for measuring student learning.

COURSE ACTIVITIES USED TO MEASURE INQUIRY QUESTION: Homework/assignment; quiz; project.

INQUIRY PRESENTATION INCLUDES: Self-reflection; example of student work; example of student essay; copy of homework assignment; excerpts from course syllabus.

ABOUT THE COURSE

My classroom inquiry focuses on a capstone course, High School Mathematics from an Advanced Standpoint, for pre-service and in-service high school mathematics education students and teachers. Exhibit 5.1 offers some details of my course. The course is designed to help students apply what is taught in their college mathematics courses to gain a deeper understanding of and connection to the various topics taught in high school mathematics. Up to this point in their education, most of my students feel that their college mathematics courses have been disconnected journeys into advanced mathematics that have little to do with their teaching. This course starts with the topics they will be teaching and then, by applying selected items from the college mathematics curriculum, uncovers the connections between the two and thereby brings them to a much deeper understanding of what they will be teaching. The goal is to give them the mathematical knowledge to conduct inquiry, to help them discover their mathematical courage to ask the unanswered questions, and to rekindle their mathematical curiosity so that they become very good teachers. The course should have the same effect on current mathematics teachers: deepen understanding, support inquiry, and rekindle their curiosity, and so it is offered also as a graduate course.

EXHIBIT 5.1
Details of Gordon's Course

Discipline	Mathematics
Course	High School Mathematics from an Advanced Standpoint
Course Level	Combined fourth-year and graduate-level
Number of Students	10
Type of Course	Targeted for high school mathematics education majors and current teachers
Meeting Time	One night per week for 2.5 hours

Since this is the second time this course has been taught, it is still very much in the design stage. Fortunately, the classroom text does a wonderful job of connecting advanced college mathematics to high school mathematics. You might think that this was surely done long ago, but you would be wrong—it is new and very subtle territory. To make matters a bit more difficult, I am teaching this course using a one night per week schedule so that it is more accessible to current teachers. So I must keep them involved, thinking, creating, for 2.5 hours at night after they've already had a long day.

COMMENTARY 5.1

Since Gordon's course is relatively new, he is using his inquiry project as a means of exploring what is effective at engaging his students. By following the inquiry model, he will be able to document his exploration and refine its development so as to share with future teachers of this course. And because his course consists of current and future teachers, he is in a unique position to share his inquiry as a pedagogical model in and of itself.

DEVELOPMENT OF THE INQUIRY

There are many aspects of this course that I would like to study. But my feeling is that the students' ability to inquire and discuss is greatly reduced by their inability to accurately communicate their mathematical ideas. Most are unable to express in writing their mathematical ideas in a coherent manner. This is true even though many write reasonably well in nonmathematical topics. One of my major goals is to significantly improve their mathematical discourse, primarily through writing, but also in oral presentations. This is a fundamentally important issue. Teachers must be able to present ideas. Mathematics teachers too often undermine the success of their students by not presenting ideas in a coherent manner. Others avoid this issue by only presenting what is scripted in their text and avoiding discussion of related issues brought up by students. All this tends to dull their students' mathematical growth. I feel that more reflective practice will help.

Mathematical discourse is not easy. The nature is that often one is expressing ideas not fully understood. Once one overcomes the uncomfortable feeling of not knowing the answers, one is able to experience the excitement of discovering new understanding and new connections. I have been reasonably successful carrying this out in my department's third-year level MATH 300: Math for Elementary Education Majors course. In this course, students have a weekly essay problem to solve or attempt to solve. The students must explain the strategies used and either explain why their solution is complete or what they feel might be missing. About half are to be done individually, although discussions with the other students is encouraged. The remainder are group assignments with a single write-up per each group of two to four students. As a result, the students' writing, seriousness, and problem-solving skills improve dramatically. While this has worked well in MATH 300, this is probably partially due to students also taking a mathematics methods course and a practicum experience during the same term.

I hope that adding essay homework assignments will work with my secondary mathematics students. My course differs from MATH 300 in several significant ways. It is not part of a block of courses. The students are not by and large afraid of mathematics, but instead are reasonably confident that they know what mathematics needs to be taught and how to teach it, and they don't see much connection with most of their college mathematics courses. The class met once a week for 2.5 hours instead of twice for 1.25 hours. I thus need to find a way to keep the discussions going throughout the rest of the week and to have the students writing about mathematics and their problem solving.

COMMENTARY 5.2

Like many teachers, Gordon used a classroom approach that he has found successful in a different course. By sharing the details of the other course that he has used as a model and by differentiating between the two courses, he allows the reader to see how he will develop his classroom inquiry. Because his new course met only once a week, Gordon was also interested in developing out-of-class components that would deepen and sustain student learning throughout the week. Gordon's discussion of mathematics discourse demonstrates his understanding that various disciplines have different rules and norms for writing—what is commonly described in academia as "discourse communities." Thus, his focus on improving students' writing and oral communication skills is grounded in criteria that he feels are reflective of successful math discourse.

PUTTING THE ISSUE INTO CONTEXT

My classroom inquiry focuses on having students attempt to solve a weekly essay homework assignment that consists of a problem or several closely related problems. Exhibit 5.2 shares 2 of the 11 problems assigned during the term. Students are required to describe their attempt, offer a justification as to its reasonableness, and argue as to whether or not they have obtained a solution. They are allowed to discuss their work and solutions with other class members. About half of the assignments are to be written up individually and the rest are a product of their group consisting of two or three students. The problems involve investigation and logical skills. None are what I would consider routine.

EXHIBIT 5.2

Examples of 2 of the 11 Essay Homework Problems

Essay Homework 1

What is the maximum and minimum number of regions you can form in the plane with 4 lines? With 5 lines? With 10 lines? Write up your result carefully. Try hard to justify why your maximum and minimum are just that.

Essay Homework 7

In the following diagram $U = 1+2i$, $w = 3+i$, M is the midpoint of the segment from U to W, V is the point that is $1/3$ of the way along this segment, Z is on the perpendicular, and length of segment V to Z is equal to that of the segment V to W. Finally, the segment from M to E has length twice that of segment U to W.

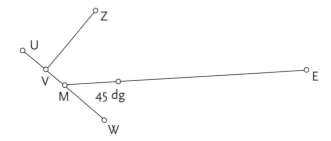

1. Find M, V, Z, and E.
2. The circle of radius 4 centered at the origin can be expressed as $|z| = 4$. Find a similar expression for the circle of radius 2 centered at $(1,3)$.
3. Describe the solution set to $|z - z_1| + |z - z_2| = 4$, where z_1 and z_2 are fixed distinct points and $4 > |z_1 - z_2|$.

4. Let A be a set of points in the plane and P be a fixed point. Rotate A about P through an angle of s radians to obtain the set B. Express B in terms of P and the points in A. Now apply this to find the set obtained by rotating the graph of $f(x) = x^3 - 2x^2 + 1$ about $(1,2)$ an angle of $1/3$ radians.

5. Consider the ellipse given by $|z - (1+i)| + |z - (2+3i)| = 10$. Now rotate this ellipse $p/3$ radians about the point $P = -1 + 2i$ to get a new ellipse. Find points w_1, w_2, and real number r so this new ellipse satisfies the equation $|w - w_1| + |w - w_2| = r$.

In their previous mathematics courses, my students were used to a weekly assignment where they applied some mathematical method or sequence of methods to a typical problem and obtained an answer. The answer was correct if they applied the correct sequence, correctly. In general, they would discuss possible approaches and compare answers, but they seldom had to justify their approach, their logic, and almost never had to convince others that they had a correct answer. This is like the difference between reciting a recipe and discussing what effect x amount of ingredient y will have on the outcome. In my course, the essay problems required the students to discuss the "ingredients," both orally and in writing. I offered a critique of their work and showed them examples of what I expected them to do. My hope was that many of these examples would come from their peers.

COMMENTARY 5.3

Gordon's recipe analogy allows readers not familiar with mathematics an insight into what he is doing and what he wants students to achieve. Think about how you can add similar analogies and examples to your work so that your inquiry is understandable to a wider audience of readers.

INQUIRY HYPOTHESIS

My hypothesis is: *A weekly essay homework problem will significantly improve the students' ability to write and discuss mathematical concepts in an accurate and coherent manner. In addition, the students will value various approaches for solving problems.*

COMMENTARY 5.4

A complicating factor that Gordon identified at the beginning of his inquiry is its once-a-week format. Gordon did not choose to address this issue here, but it might give rise to a future inquiry. Such courses pose a number of challenges, not only because of the 2.5-hour length but also because they are more likely to contain a mix of traditional and nontraditional students or of "professionals in training" and "experienced professionals." In Gordon's class, he had a mix of future teachers and those who were already full-time teachers.

INVESTIGATIVE PLAN

In my use of weekly essay homework assignments in my previous MATH 300 course, I saw a significant improvement in student confidence and ability by mid-semester. I expected a similar occurrence in this course. My main source of data would be copies of the classroom work of the 10 students collected over the entire term. This included their essay problems, quizzes, text problems, and any group projects that they were part of. From my course syllabus, Exhibit 5.3 describes the different types of course activities and my expectations for each.

EXHIBIT 5.3

Description of the Range of Classroom Activities and Gordon's Expectations

ESSAY HOMEWORK (10 pts): *Group produced.* Carefully write up solutions in good English form. Pay particular attention to mathematical details, coherence, readability, and correctness. Justify your answers with clear explanations. Give logical explanations for your attempts even if you cannot solve a question. I have included all the essay homework problems. Seventy percent of the grade is based on the writing and correct use of the mathematics, including terms.

TEXTBOOK HOMEWORK (10 pts): *Group produced.* Show serious attempt to solve the problem. Show work. Need only provide a summary justification of the work. There are typically 6–10 problems that range from elementary to advanced interpretations of terminology and methods to problems that require mature ingenuity. Eighty percent of grade is based on evidence of serious attempt to do the problems.

READING QUIZ (2 pts): *Individually produced.* A check to promote actually doing the assigned reading and another encouragement to write carefully. These were primarily definitions and statements of theorems. Two points means that the definition is correct and well written.

MAJOR PROJECTS: Thoroughly cover the topic. Find connections with other concepts in the course. Look for other mathematical connections with courses you've had. Write up your findings in a report form. Explain the mathematics and mathematical connections carefully when appropriate (some of the connections require much more advanced work and are not expected here). Give references. Fifty percent of the grade is the writing and 50% is the mathematics (accurate use of terms, justifications, connections, correction definitions, etc.)

COMMENTARY 5.5

Gordon focuses his data collection on examples of his students' work. This data collection will be useful for tracking their development and growth. While his hypothesis suggests that he is also interested in exploring how students value various problem-solving approaches, his data probably will not provide him with the answer to this question. In order to more fully address his hypothesis, he might have examined other aspects of his course, such as:

- *Some measure of students' growth in being able to talk about concepts.* Since oral communication in mathematics discourse is one of Gordon's interests, he could track the level and improvement in his students' abilities to present and discuss their work. To do so, he could have an outside observer evaluate one or more of his class discussions. Or Gordon could self-evaluate each classroom discussion immediately after class, perhaps with the aid of a formal rubric.
- *Some measure of students' perceptions of the impact.* He could ask students if they thought their abilities and skills had developed as a result of the essay homework, either through a student survey or through written reflection.

INTERPRETING AND EVALUATING FINDINGS

My plan was to collect copies of the first two sets of essay homework and reading quizzes and the last couple of sets and then compare the two. I had hoped that the group discussions necessary to complete the assignments would help students to appreciate different approaches to solving a particular problem. But in a rush to return the first few assignments, I forgot or didn't have time to make copies. So, I started with the fourth set and collected sets 4 to 7 and 9. Sets 8 and 10 did not include essay homework because major projects were due those weeks.

COMMENTARY 5.6

Gordon originally planned to keep copies of all of the student work required for the class. Because he had only 10 students, this plan was feasible. Still, due to the number of different assignments involved, Gordon was placing a significant amount of work on himself. In the chaos of the first few weeks this plan fell through. Having to revise one's collection plan is not unusual. Teaching does not occur in a vacuum, and numerous factors (some that we control, many that we do not) may lead us to change data collection methods after the course begins. In Gordon's case, he quickly reassessed and moved on. One strategy that might have alleviated this problem would be requiring students to keep their own course portfolios. For example, you grade and return each assignment to your students and they add it to their class portfolio. At the end of the term, they turn in this complete portfolio (and possibly receive some nominal number of course points). This would simplify data collection since you would make copies of student work only at the end of the term rather than on a weekly (or daily) basis. Also, having students create an archive of their own work is an effective tool for them to reflect on their growth and development at the end of the course.

As I evaluated the essay assignments, I found that they were poorly written to start with, but by the fourth all were pretty good. Exhibit 5.4 is a copy of part of a student's solution to essay homework 7. This was a technical problem dealing with the relations between complex numbers, vectors, and complex arithmetic. In my inquiry course portfolio (available at www.courseportfolio.org), I include the complete student solution from Exhibit 5.4 along with the complete solutions of two additional students.

EXHIBIT 5.4

Student Solution to Essay Homework 7

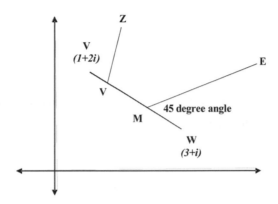

The graph above is in the copletx plane with $U = 1 + 2i$ and $W = 3 + i$. M is the midpoint of $\overline{UW}$, V is 1/3 of the way along $\overline{UW}$, Z is n the perpendicular to $\overline{UW}$ with $UW = 2V$ and $WME = 45°$ and $ME = 2UW$

Since M is the midpoint of $\overline{UW}$,

$$M = \frac{U + W}{2} = \frac{(1 + 2i) + (3 + i)}{2} = \frac{4 + 3i}{2} = 2 + \frac{3}{2}i$$

To find V, first find the segment from U to W. This is $-U + W$. Since V is 1/3 along this segment, adding 1/3 of $-U + W$ to V produced V:

$$V = \frac{1}{3}(-U + W) + U = \frac{1}{3}(-(1 + 2i) + (3 + i)) + (1 + 2i) = \frac{5}{3} + \frac{5}{3}i$$

M can also be found using this way:

$$M = \frac{1}{2}(-U + W) + U = \frac{1}{2}(2 - i) + (1 + 2i) = 2 + \frac{3}{2}i$$

This verifies the earlies method of calucating M

In my inquiry course portfolio, I also included three graded quizzes for a sample of four students. Exhibit 5.5 shares an example of one student's solution. As I followed my students' progress, I saw improvement in the writing, more complete sentences, fewer vague terms, and clearer separation of the statements. As an example of students' development, the reading quizzes for Student 1 show a marked writing improvement in quizzes 5 and 6 when compared to quiz 3. The same is true for Student 7. Quiz 3 for Student 2 made no sense while quizzes 5 and 6 are much better, even though the answer to 6 is wrong. Students 2 and 4 already wrote pretty well in all three of the quizzes included in my complete inquiry.

EXHIBIT 5.5

Student Solution to Reading Quiz 3

A number r is algebraic when the polynomial $p(x)$ has coefficients such that r is the root of $p(x) = 0$.

In my complete inquiry portfolio, I also include copies of the major project for two groups of students—an example of a "high-pass" project and one of a "low-pass" project. Both are well written. The low pass messed up on some definitions, left some terms undefined, did not explain the significance of the graph, and had some incorrect table labels—all of which might indicate the group did not plan enough time to proof their work. My main complaint about the low-pass project is that the students did not show connections or even attempt to discuss the mathematics in the methods they were describing.

COMMENTARY 5.7

Gordon chose to demonstrate the impact of his essay homework by showcasing actual examples of student work from his course. For brevity's sake, only a small sample of what he included in his inquiry course portfolio (described in Chapter 11) is included here. Gordon's full inquiry project can be examined at www.courseport-folio.org. Complementing the student examples is his reflective assessment of how students developed. Gordon used rather broad statements about how students improved over time, although this may not be noticed by someone outside the mathematics discipline. The presentation could be strengthened if he had included a range of student performance (e.g., grades) on the classroom assessments. For example, a graph showing how students' grades developed over the term would illustrate the improvement in student learning in a visual fashion. Throughout his reflection, Gordon articulates his criteria for what constitutes effective mathematics discourse, but he does not say whether he shared these criteria with students during the term. Now that he has articulated these criteria, he can use them in future offerings of the course. He can also provide students with essay homework examples and discuss why they are or are not effective—an example of how inquiry into a course can cycle back into pedagogical improvement.

FINAL REFLECTION

The big question is: *Does the data support my hypothesis?* Well, this is a bit awkward. I don't have examples of the students' earliest work to show this. My recollection of their early work is that they did improve considerably, but the proof is not here. There is another difference between the early work and that which is displayed in my portfolio. Essay homework 1 and 2 were problems that the students had to solve. Not only were the solutions a bit difficult, but justifying that the solutions were really correct was also not easy. Essay homework 3 was too long. In the remaining essay homework, it was fairly obvious what one needed to do. This might have allowed the students more thinking time to devote to their actual writing.

COMMENTARY 5.8

Notice how Gordon reflects on the different level of effort and skills needed for each of the essay homework assignments. In retrospect, it may be a good thing that he did not collect copies of the first few assignments as he had planned. As Gordon points out, these assignments differed qualitatively from later assignments, which would have made his strategy of comparing them more difficult. Unless you have taught a course several times (this was only the second time Gordon had taught this course), it is hard to envision the exact form and format of the classroom assignments until you are already in the process of teaching the course. The inquiry process, however, led Gordon to see these key differences in his essay homework, providing him with useful information for revising the essay prompts for his next course offering. Another method that Gordon might have used to measure improvement over the semester would have been to use a pre-test and post-test. For instance, he could have had students complete the same or very similar writing assignments at the beginning, and then again at the end of the term. This process would have allowed him to measure the impact of the course on student skills more directly.

As a result of my classroom inquiry, I have given considerable thought to having my students do reflective writing about their own learning, especially after reading the classroom inquiry work of Dana Fritz (Chapter 2). I still believe that carefully written presentations are important for several reasons: to improve the accuracy and completeness of their oral presentations (i.e., teaching presentations); to aid in the development of understanding of the concepts; and to aid in finding connections with previous mathematics the students have encountered. But there needs to be more reflection on the students' part about their own learning. I need to make sure the students understand why I am asking them to write, and I need to convince them to take on writing as an important part of their training to be effective teachers. I also need more individual writing assignments to ensure that all are benefiting from the process. Finally, I need to define clearly what items I will collect to support the hypothesis that my practices will enable the students to improve their writing during the course and help them appreciate a variety of approaches.

COMMENTARY 5.9

Gordon's reflection on his students' writing performance helps him articulate an important learning goal that his current inquiry does not address: student understanding about the importance of writing for mathematics teachers. While Gordon's inquiry collects data that examines whether or not students writing improved, it does not collect information regarding his students' perceptions about the value of writing in relation to their teacher training preparation. Since some of Gordon's students are current mathematics teachers, it would be especially interesting to see how they view writing in their professional lives and to gauge the extent to which they already incorporate writing as a tool in their own teaching. Such information could easily be collected through several methods, such as a survey, a written journal, an electronic forum, or a class discussion.

To this end, when I teach this course again, I will have small individual writing assignments to be developed in groups. These will be assigned by Thursday morning with each member of a group having different problems assigned to them. The students will post their first draft to their group on the web-based academic portal (Blackboard) by Saturday morning for a critique. Each group member will critique each other's posting by Monday morning. Then each will use the critiques to write a final version of their solution and post it. I will grade the final version and the critiques.

I will need to create a rubric for the individual writing, for the critique, and for the group response to the homework. I will also indicate by Saturday morning who will be orally presenting which homework problems to the class that coming Wednesday. This information will give these students time to consult with me if they are having difficulties. The oral presentations often bring out solutions different from those turned in by other groups. Other times I bring up different ways of doing the problems and we discuss the various approaches in class. This format should help them appreciate the value of different methods for solving a problem.

The bottom line is that I want to keep the students engaged by having them present their work, being responsible for developing a good presentation, having them look for connections with other areas of mathematics, and having them help their classmates learn—much like the teachers they hope to become.

COMMENTARY 5.10

We actually disagree with Gordon's statement that he did not prove his hypothesis. The level of proof required is highly dependent on what you intend to do with your classroom inquiry work. In Gordon's case, the inquiry was for his own development as a teacher. By documenting and tracking his inquiry, he created a record of what his students accomplished. Could he have done his inquiry better? Of course—but this is true of most classroom inquiries. The key is that his analysis was useful to him and provided him with answers to significant questions he had about his course. In fact, his reflection on those answers has led him to realize that he is missing the student voice in assessing the assignments' impact on student learning. This realization was developed through his reading about the classroom inquiry work of others. By completing his classroom inquiry project, Gordon has identified a future inquiry issue and has even mapped out a plan for exploring it. By posing a question, answering it, and cycling the results back into the course, Gordon is well under way on his journey as a scholarly teacher.

CHAPTER SIX

LINKING CLASSROOM INQUIRY WITH DISCIPLINARY RESEARCH

My inquiry has forced me to develop clear-cut course goals and objectives that have now been defined in such a way that I can measure them. Along with showing me how to self-evaluate my classroom, my inquiry project has also helped to link my teaching with my disciplinary research.

—D'ANDRA OREY

INQUIRY OVERVIEW: D'Andra explores whether increased use of supplementary materials related to race will lead to an increase in racial tolerance among students in his first-year political science course. He also asks whether there is a difference in attitudes of tolerance between students in the Honors section of his course versus those in the non-Honors section.

HIGHLIGHTS: Teaching and research can be closely connected, as we bring insights from our own research into the classroom or involve our students in research projects. D'Andra's inquiry is influenced by his own research in two ways. First, he assesses the impact of his treatment of issues of race and politics on student attitudes, then he compares receptivity to issues of race among different groups of students. In keeping with his social science background, D'Andra uses a quantitative survey and statistical analysis to assess the impact of materials about race on students' attitudes. His data does not yield the results he had hoped for, but it does give him a deeper understanding of his students and generates some useful ideas about how he can change his teaching to improve student learning.

COURSE ACTIVITIES USED TO MEASURE INQUIRY QUESTION: Homework/assignment; pre-assessment, post-assessment.

Inquiry presentation includes: Self-reflection; data table; statistical analysis; example of student essay; copy of student survey; excerpts from course syllabus.

ABOUT THE COURSE

Power and Politics is an introductory course designed to provide students with a broad overview of the American political system. Exhibit 6.1 shares details of my course. The course is not a survey of American history. Some students come to the course with strong history backgrounds; however, they soon learn that political science and history, although overlapping in content, are two separate fields of study. Politics, no matter how much people perceive it to be boring subject matter, is a very salient topic in the United States. Students often enter my course with their own preconceived notions and explanations of political phenomena. Given this fact, one of the goals of this course is to strongly encourage students to learn how to think critically and analytically about the political process. To attain this goal, I attempt to place the course within the broader context of political science as a discipline, whereby the emphasis is on *science*.

EXHIBIT 6.1
Details of D'Andra's Course

Discipline	Political Science
Course	Power and Politics
Course Level	First-year
Number of Students	43 (21 students in an Honors section and 22 in a non-Honors section)
Type of Course	Required course for political science majors, but because it has no prerequisite, it attracts a diverse mix of students
Meeting Time	One night per week for 2.5 hours along with a once-a-week 50-minute recitation session

---

Given my research interests, I have attempted to incorporate race and gender as a substantive means for discussing politics in the course, particularly as it relates to "who gets what, when and how." In doing so, there is a possibility that some students may complete the course feeling that the focus of the class was the actual substantive nature of the discussion as opposed to the more abstract theoretical frameworks introduced in the text. This approach proves to be more problematic with discussions of race, given the homogeneous racial setting of the school (and state) in which I teach. These problems notwithstanding, another course goal is to provide students with a different perspective/context for which to critically analyze the political system. Arguably, encouraging students to think from a different perspective ("outside the box") helps to improve their overall critical and analytical thinking skills.

COMMENTARY 6.1

Rather then complete his classroom inquiry in isolation from his disciplinary research, D'Andra is exploring how the two intersect. D'Andra's observation that some students view substantive discussions about race, rather than the abstract theoretical framework of political science, as the primary subject of the course provides him with the "problem" that he wants to analyze. To pursue this question further, he will focus on one topic taught within the course—that of race—rather than looking at course content as a whole.

DEVELOPMENT OF THE INQUIRY

Teaching students about race and politics at a traditionally white school has proven to be a challenge. But to be fair, teaching American government/politics in general (without focusing on race) proves to be problematic for any teacher because, well . . . everybody "thinks" that they know politics. For example, I can recall sitting at a luncheon amidst an interdisciplinary crowd when a very close friend from another discipline gave his theory of how the Democratic presidential primary winner would be chosen. His source unfortunately was Bill Maher, former host of the now-defunct show *Politically Incorrect*. Admittedly, I actually enjoyed the few episodes that I watched; however, this show is a very unreliable source for receiving a credible perspective on winning the Democratic primary. Typically, we political scientists turn to presidential or election scholars. Like my colleague, many students enter my introductory course with what are considered "doorstep" opinions (i.e., made up on the spot). I describe these opinions in the "overview" section of my course syllabus (Exhibit 6.2).

Exhibit 6.2
Excerpt From D'Andra's Course Syllabus

Unfortunately, similar to the Monday morning (Sunday morning for college football fans) quarterback, politics is a field whereby many citizens have self-proclaimed themselves as experts, depending on which beauty salon/barber shop or bar they frequent. Hence, this course seeks to reduce the number of "doorstep" opinions by teaching students how to systematically search for the truth (i.e., carve away as much residual to get as close to the truth as possible) as it relates to the field of politics. The course will also place strong emphasis on positivist questions, which address "what is?" as opposed to the normative approach, which addresses "what ought to be?"

By focusing on empirical evidence from a positivist rather than a normative approach, students are forced to support their intuitions or general notions with facts. This approach helps to minimize the role of emotions in contentious discussions. In some cases, such a demand poses a problem for students because the evidence that they find does not fit with their prior notions, particularly on issues regarding race. This experience might cause the student to reject the incoming information altogether, regardless of the source. Such behavior is known as *cognitive dissonance.* Cognitive dissonance has been defined as an "inconsistency among related beliefs" (Jones & Gerard, 1967, p. 42). According to Jones and Gerard, this inconsistency leads to a "motivation to do whatever is easiest in order to regain cognitive consistency or consonance among beliefs" (p. 42). Hence, because the student is unable to engage in intellectual discourse at the level of abstraction presented by the instructor, he or she will simply dismiss the presentation as inaccurate, mythical, or simply false.

COMMENTARY 6.2

One of the issues D'Andra faces in teaching this course is students' preconceptions about the field of political science—students think they already know a lot about the subject. This is not an uncommon phenomenon in many general survey courses, and helping eliminate misconceptions can be as important a task for the teacher as conveying new information. By sharing the discussion of "doorstep" opinions from his syllabus, D'Andra shows readers how

> he makes his students aware at the very beginning of the term that learning to distinguish facts from opinions and prescriptions will be an important part of his course.

PUTTING THE ISSUE INTO CONTEXT

The purpose of my inquiry is to determine when substantive discussions of race and gender may, in fact, be too much. I chose this topic because, inevitably, on previous course evaluations at least one student indicated that the course focused too much on topics relating to race. Despite my equal focus on issues pertaining to gender, I have never had a student suggest that the course focused too much on women. Whether or not these students constitute a minority, I believe that this is an important research question and therefore deserves serious inquiry.

INQUIRY HYPOTHESIS

I have two hypotheses for my inquiry. The first hypothesis is: *An increase in exposure to ancillary materials related to race will lead to an increase in racial tolerance.* This hypothesis is posited because it will shed some light on how much is too much. In other words, if students possess high levels of negative racial attitudes, it may not be a good idea to provide too many substantive examples that are rooted in race. While one could advance the argument that this is the very reason that more materials should be covered pertaining to race, one has to keep in mind that race is not the main focus of my course. Since I am teaching two sections of the same course—one an Honors section and one a non-Honors section—my second hypothesis is: *Students in my Honors course will possess more racially tolerant attitudes when compared to students in my non-Honors course.*

COMMENTARY 6.3

D'Andra's concern that the course's focus on race is "too much" for students considers the role of "affect" in students' learning. He wants to investigate the relationship between students' attitudes toward race and their engagement in the course material. Thus, his focus is not on examining actual student performance but rather on determining whether and to what extent he can change students' attitudes on a specific issue, in this case race and its role in politics.

INVESTIGATIVE PLAN

The data for my classroom inquiry are derived from two sources: 1) a survey administered to both sections (Honors and non-Honors) of my course; and 2) examples from a student writing assignment after students have read Peggy McIntosh's (1988) essay, "White Privilege: Unpacking the Invisible Knapsack." In the Honors section there are 21 students and in the non-Honors section there are 22 students. As an aside, I should mention that all of the students in my courses are white. In fact, in the three previous occasions I have taught this course, I have had a total of one student of color take it.

COMMENTARY 6.4

D'Andra's analysis will measure changes in attitudes about race within the course of a semester. A much more difficult question to answer would be the long-term or lasting effect of the course on student attitudes.

The survey questions are adopted from the political science literature on racial attitudes. A brief digression is necessary here to provide some background regarding these items. The concept of racial resentment has been described as a mutation from the old-fashioned overt racism of yesterday, to a new and more subtle racism. In other words, whites no longer express the belief that blacks are biologically inferior to whites; instead, they express anti-black emotions blended with the belief that blacks fail to adhere to traditional American values such as individualism, hard work, discipline, and the American ethos of self-help.

In recent years, social scientists have constructed public opinion surveys to help capture this so-called new racism around the following dimensions: 1) resentment about special favors for blacks; 2) denial of continuing discrimination; 3) belief that blacks should work harder; and 4) excessive demands. Exhibit 6.3 outlines typical questions used. The resentment scale is a continuous scale coded from 0 to 1. The low end of the scale represents racial tolerance, whereas the high end of the scale represents resentment. In addition to survey items tapping racial resentment toward blacks, thermometer scales are also employed. These items range from 0 to 100, with 0 representing a cool attachment to the group and 100 representing a hot or close alignment with the group.

EXHIBIT 6.3

Example Questions for Measuring Racial Resentment

Resentment About Special Favors for Blacks
QUESTION: *Over the past few years, blacks have gotten less than they deserve.*
Respondents who disagree with this statement are placed in the racial resentment category.

Denial of Continuing Discrimination
QUESTION: *Generations of slavery and discrimination have created conditions that make it difficult for blacks to work their way out of the lower class.*
Respondents who disagree with this statement are placed in the racial resentment category.

Blacks Should Work Harder
QUESTION 1: *Irish, Italians, Jewish, and many other minorities overcame prejudice and worked their way up. Blacks should do the same without special favors.*

QUESTION 2: *It's really a matter of some people not trying hard enough; if blacks would only try harder they could be just as well off as whites.*
Respondents who agree with these statements are placed into the racial resentment category.

In an effort to test the first hypothesis, that an increase in substantive materials on race will increase racial tolerance, I will administer my survey before and after the students' exposure to these materials. In particular, I will examine the responses to the resentment scales before exposure and after exposure. I will use also a statistical test (difference of means test) to measure results. The second hypothesis is not tested using a statistical test; however, I will compare and contrast the survey results for the Honors and non-Honors sections of the course.

COMMENTARY 6.5

D'Andra shares some useful details of his data collection, including a description of the survey instrument he will use and how he is going to analyze the results. Rather than including the lengthy survey in his inquiry, he shares sample questions, so that readers know the types of items students will be asked. His presentation might be more helpful if he shared more detail about the substantive materials he planned to use and at what point in the course he was going to introduce them. Readers might also appreciate more information about the student writing assignment.

INTERPRETING AND EVALUATING FINDINGS

The result of the statistical test (Exhibit 6.4) fails to support my first hypothesis. That is, an increase in substantive materials on race had no impact on racial attitudes between the time of the first and the second survey. The difference of mean responses between the two surveys is only 0.011, too small to have statistical significance. There are a couple of potential explanations for these findings. First, Honors students were used in this analysis, and based on their mean scores, these students expressed somewhat low levels of racial animus toward blacks prior to the classroom discussions. Hence, it is highly likely that these students may have already been exposed to similar materials earlier in their academic career and thus additional exposure was not likely to increase their scores significantly. Second, the time lapse between administration of the first and the second survey may not have been long enough.

EXHIBIT 6.4

Difference in Means Statistic Test Between the
Pre-Survey and Post-Survey Results

Mean Difference	Standard Deviation	Standard Error Mean	95% Lower Confidence Interval	95% Upper Confidence Internal	t	df	Significance (2-tailed)
-.01136	0.18056	0.03850	-0.09142	0.06869	-0.295	21	0.771

Exhibit 6.5 lends support to my second hypothesis, showing that Honors students, on average, scored lower on the racial resentment scale when compared to non-Honors students. With regard to attitudes toward out-groups, my first cut at the data suggested that non-Honors students scored higher than the Honors students on measures of resentment toward blacks and Hispanics. It appears that these results run counter to my aforementioned hypothesis. Upon closer scrutiny, however, I found that Honors students were also more likely to have lower scores for whites than were non-Honors students.

EXHIBIT 6.5

Racial Attitudes of Honors and Non-Honors Students

	Mean Honors Section	Mean Non-Honors Section
Resentment	0.23	0.58
Whites thermometer	68.2	79.5
Blacks thermometer	67.7	71.5
Hispanic thermometer	64.8	68.2
White–blacks	0.48	8
White—Hispanic	3.43	11.3
Sample size	21	22

As a result of these findings, I decided to take the difference between each respondent's "temperature" or alignment score for their in-group (whites) and for each of the minority groups (blacks and Hispanics). This method achieved different results. The average difference in scores given to blacks is very close to the scores given to whites. Honors students align themselves a bit more closely to blacks than to Hispanics, but the difference is still marginal when compared to non-Honors students. Numerically, the average difference between the Honors students' alignment with whites is within a point of that given to blacks. This compares to an 8-point difference for non-Honors students. Likewise, the difference in scores between their in-group and Hispanics is approximately

3.43 points for Honors students and more than 10 points for non-Honors students. These results are consistent with my hypothesis that Honors students exhibit more racially tolerant attitudes than do non-Honors students.

COMMENTARY 6.6

D'Andra has used statistical analysis of his survey results to evaluate his two hypotheses. His statistical test and numerical comparisons are appropriate and valid, and D'Andra does a good job of explaining the results in relation to his hypotheses questions. Because political scientists frequently use statistics in their research, his approach to analyzing the data will seem familiar to many. To readers from disciplines that do not use statistical techniques, his analysis might be a bit overwhelming. As you plan your own inquiry, you should ask yourself how an audience from outside your discipline might react to your presentation.

My findings based on the student writing are mixed. Student 1 (Exhibit 6.6) appears to be frustrated by the assignment and somewhat put off. She interprets the author's white privilege argument as implying that all whites are racists. In the second paragraph she states clearly that she is bothered by the author's comments. As a result of the student's frustrations, she fails to complete the assignment of comparing and contrasting the two concepts at hand. While not reproduced here, in my inquiry course portfolio (www.courseportfolio.org) I include copies of three additional student papers. Of these, Students 2 and 3 reveal that the assignment was the first time that they had received exposure to such materials and that it really made them rethink some of their original policy positions. In fact, the title of Student 3's essay is "An Unlikely Supporter." Here, the student refers to affirmative action. Lastly, Student 4 indicates that her exposure to a guest speaker during MLK (Martin Luther King, Jr.) week helped her to better understand race relations. To be sure, the sample size of the qualitative data is small; however, the findings are still useful for future research.

EXHIBIT 6.6
Sample of Student's Paper

PoliSci 100H
White privilege/reaction paper

After reading the article on while privilege, I am feeling a bit awkward. On the one hand, I am slightly incensed at the thought that every white person is racist simply because they were white, but on the other, the author does make a valid point. There is the problem of minority disadvantage being equal to white advantage. However, some of the points that the author makes are less credible in my eyes. Things such as 'band-aids are my color of skin' and 'I can buy posers, dolls, and trading cars with my race represented' are ludicrous at best. I, personally, enjoy using neon colored band-aids although my skin is definitively not neon pink. There are also many famous minority athletes (especially in football and basketball) and it is possible to easily find dolls of any race. More importantly, I fail to see how having band-aids in a certain color gives me a definite advantage over someone else. However, some ideas by the author 'obtaining a hob with an affirmative action employers' and 'if I am pulled over by a cop, I know it's not because of my race' are true, and the difference between the races in this cases are a problem. However, the claim that I am racist simply because I'm not a minority is slightly infuriating.

The problem here is that one person cannot chance an entire race. It bothers me that although I treat people of minorities exactly the same as others, I'm still a terrible, terrible person because I was born to white parents. I agree that yes, there is a standard of white privilege. However, I, myself cannot end it alone. For most of this article, I get the idea that the author wants whites to give up their privileges so that they are equal to minorities.

COMMENTARY 6.7

D'Andra's analysis of the four student papers (for brevity sake, only one is included here) feels a bit incomplete. The analysis would have been clearer to readers if D'Andra had explained the writing assignment in as much detail as he did the survey measures that he used. *What was the goal of the assignment? How was it connected to his understanding of students' racial tolerance? When was it administered? What criteria were used to evaluate it?*

> In addition, while D'Andra offers reflective commentary on the examples that he highlights, he does not set these examples into the larger context by explaining how they fit within the entire group of 43 students. D'Andra might have included a graph or summary of his grades for this assignment. Or he might have classified the responses according to the percentage of students whose writing demonstrated varying degrees ("much," "some," "little," "none," or "negative") of impact on their beliefs.

FINAL REFLECTION

The findings from my classroom inquiry create a dilemma. It appears that non-Honors students are in greater need of exposure to topics pertaining to race in comparison to Honors students. This inference is based solely on the results of my comparison of racial attitudes. Given that prior research suggests that students might engage in cognitive dissonance, it is recommended here that such topics be withheld from the introductory courses and incorporated into higher-level courses. The argument here is that the teacher may have to engage in too much unraveling of stereotypes and myths that might have been developed during pre-adult socialization periods. As a result, the course might end up being inadvertently diverted into a course on race and politics.

At first glance, one might see such discussions as unnecessary for the Honors students, given their higher levels of tolerance when compared to non-Honors students. Similarly, one could envision such a strategy as "preaching to the choir." Despite the high levels of tolerance possessed by the Honors students, it has been my experience that even Honors students possess high levels of stereotypes and myths that can easily be dispelled with empirical evidence. This evidence often leads to the highest level of intellectual exchange during the course. Hence, while I suggest that research on race be kept to a minimum for non-Honors Power and Politics students, I highly recommend that Honors students receive as much as the course will permit, without the course being perceived as a course on race.

COMMENTARY 6.8

D'Andra's inquiry has demonstrated the differing levels of racial tolerance between Honors and non-Honors students, while his past experience has shown him both the need to address issues of race and the benefits of such discussion with Honors students. Given the constraints of this particular course, a general survey of political science, he has concluded that an in-depth examination of race would best be restricted to the Honors students, where the topic can be developed more fully. Although this may seem to be a "negative" conclusion, D'Andra's inquiry has given him valuable information that will influence what materials and topics he does—and does not—include the next time he teaches the course. His inquiry has also generated new questions about how to integrate discussions of racial attitudes into the Honors section of the course, which in turn could be the subject of further inquiry. For instance, *would a different set of readings or a different type of writing assignment have provoked a different reaction?* Or, as D'Andra suggests next, perhaps he should broaden his discussion of racial issues.

One way to achieve this goal (in my case) is to focus on substantive issues beyond African-Americans. Based on the thermometer scores, there is an equal, if not greater, need to address issues pertaining to Hispanics. Given the geographical location of our school, the same need exists for discussions regarding Native Americans.

Lastly, issues pertaining to gender have always been received better than issues related to race. The idea here is not to eliminate discussions pertaining to race, for that would defeat the purpose of incorporating diversity into one's teaching. The goal is to find that perfect mix of diverse topics, without losing any students.

COMMENTARY 6.9

D'Andra's venture into linking his disciplinary research on race and gender with his classroom has given him new insights into the effectiveness of his teaching. As he acknowledges at the beginning of his inquiry, discussions about race bring out perceptions and beliefs that are hard to change. D'Andra has not given up on his goal of challenging students to examine their "doorstep" opinions, but he has learned that his current method of approaching the issue of race is not as successful as he had thought. His inquiry has resulted in more specific information about student attitudes and caused him to think about broadening his presentation of this topic within the course by looking at several minority groups and at issues of gender as well as of race. Like all successful inquiries, this one has generated new questions that are worth pursuing further and that help D'Andra develop as a scholarly teacher.

CHAPTER SEVEN

OBTAINING USEFUL INQUIRY RESULTS, BUT MORE DATA IS NEEDED

To push the envelope in teaching is to invite risk. An inquiry project allows you to find the opportunity in the risk.

—TIM WENTZ

INQUIRY OVERVIEW: Tim asks whether there is an ideal size and team member composition that will enhance student success on a service-learning project in his third-year construction management and architecture course.

HIGHLIGHTS: Tim is interested in exploring how best to promote success on a project that involves student teams. His inquiry focuses on the composition of the teams, examining how many and what types of students comprise the most effective teams. Tim's population of construction management and architecture majors poses interesting conflicts that are replicated within the professional industry settings in which his students will later work. Tim feels that he is unable to answer his hypothesis fully at the end of the inquiry. But his inquiry has given him new insight into how student groups function, and he knows that he is on the right track to answering his question.

COURSE ACTIVITIES USED TO MEASURE INQUIRY QUESTION: Project; examination; student peer critique and review; student course evaluation.

INQUIRY PRESENTATION INCLUDES: Self-reflection; student commentary; data table; photograph of student work; grading rubric.

ABOUT THE COURSE

The course I am investigating is Building Environmental Technical Systems. This cross-listed course is required for students in my department (construction management) and those from the architecture program. Exhibit 7.1 shares details of my course. Since 2003, I have taught this cross-listed course each fall and have continued to update and modify it to keep it current.

EXHIBIT 7.1
Details of Tim's Course

Discipline	Construction Management and Architecture
Course	Building Environmental Technical Systems I
Course Level	Third-year
Number of Students	87
Type of Course	A required service-learning course for construction management and architecture students
Meeting Time	Two 75-minute class sessions per week, along with a 50-minute recitation period per week

---

The course includes a team-based service-learning project. In teaching the fundamentals of mechanical systems, I have found it beneficial to have a project that students can use to apply the material presented in the classroom. Additionally, the construction industry has always used multidisciplinary teams to solve these types of problems. Accordingly, I thought this teaching methodology would have the added benefit of preparing students for the same types of team dynamics they will encounter as they enter professional practice and help them develop problem-solving skills from a team perspective. Linking the project with a community organization in need of construction and design assistance is useful for students, not only to give back to the community, but also to learn how to work under the constraints of a limited budget. As a result of focusing my course around a project, it was necessary to structure all of the lectures, homework, quizzes, and examinations around it. Moreover, the grading emphasis is distributed so that the majority of the course grade is based on the final project. Although the semester project grade is a team grade, I felt it was necessary to implement a method of peer evaluation so that the team members could apportion the grade within the team based on the amount of work and the quality of work done by each team member.

COMMENTARY 7.1

In designing his inquiry, Tim has a significant advantage because he is teaching a course for pre-professional students. His inquiry and his service-learning project focus on helping his students learn course concepts that they will apply once they graduate. In comparison, it requires much more creativity for teachers in the liberal arts to design similar real-life projects. As an aside, Tim's use of a service-learning project in such a large-size course is a testament to his comfort in using this rewarding but challenging teaching approach.

DEVELOPMENT OF THE INQUIRY

Because it is a critical component in this course, I propose to study aspects of my students' team-based learning. Not having formally investigated this issue previously, I am left with a sense that some teams perform much better than others. I am looking for those criteria that separate the good teams from underperforming ones. Some of the issues that occur to me as I start this process include team size, academic diversity, disciplinary diversity, gender diversity, and geographic diversity.

How students best learn in a team format is of great importance for a variety of reasons. From an academic standpoint, schools are moving toward larger courses in response to reductions in funding and fewer professors available to teach. This trend is especially true in my discipline. One way to overcome some of the problems inherent in large-class instruction is to break down the class into smaller groups. Developing a methodology that allows for larger courses and still increases student learning would be of tremendous benefit to me and others.

From an industry perspective, teaching students how to work within teams to produce workable solutions is equally important. Virtually all construction, engineering, and architectural projects are conducted in a team format. A teaching methodology that helps students develop team and networking skills, team problem solving, and communication skills with clients will be exciting for the industry that hires our graduates. It is also worth noting that our industry has had a long history of relationship problems between architects, engineers, and construction managers. Oftentimes, they view each other as obstacles to reaching a solution, as opposed to partners in the process. We could do the industry an immeasurable service by working to break down these barriers before the students enter the profession.

COMMENTARY 7.2

Having taught this course numerous times, Tim is well aware of the issues related to the use of group projects to improve student learning. He contextualizes his inquiry as a problem that needs to be addressed both within his industry and within higher education more generally. If Tim were interested in publishing the findings of his inquiry for these audiences, he could further bolster this section by providing evidence of these conflicts between architects, engineers, and construction managers.

From a teacher's standpoint, using a teaching methodology that incorporates "students teaching students" within the class is bound to make teaching more effective and fun. This method emphasizes the fact that teaching is a process and it really doesn't all have to flow from a single point at the front of a classroom. Solving a real-life problem through a service-learning project also addresses one of the most worrisome questions in any teacher's mind: *Are my students learning the material such that they can solve this problem in the real world?* In other words, this process really focuses on an outcome—what the students can do when they walk out of my classroom door.

Finally, from a student's perspective, team learning within a large classroom setting is bound to be more exciting if done well. Team learning removes some of the isolation that students often feel in a large course. Better yet, the isolation is removed within a team that contains students one would normally not work with, inasmuch as students from construction management and architecture don't often interact. It is not lost on the students that they are solving a real-world problem. Inherently, students want to perform well and, in my opinion, genuinely want to acquire the skills they know they will need when they enter professional practice. They have the opportunity to solve a real-world problem using this methodology with virtually no risk, other than perhaps a poor grade.

COMMENTARY 7.3

Tim states his initial assumption that students will find this project exciting and fun. One aspect of his inquiry could focus on gauging student perceptions and attitudes toward the project to see if these assumptions are accurate.

PUTTING THE ISSUE INTO CONTEXT

Although previous students have generally been very positive regarding the team-based project, some have expressed their concerns as well. For example, a number of students have complained that the smaller groups were at a competitive disadvantage because larger teams had more resources to draw on and could do more research and better distribute the workload. The result was that their proposals would be better than the smaller teams'. From my own observation, team size has been a challenge. The literature has long advocated teams of five to eight for maximum effectiveness. At the same time, many of my colleagues are hesitant to form teams that large, fearing that the less assertive, unprepared, or poorly motivated students will be left behind. As such, team size is one aspect I plan to investigate.

Another typical complaint is that some teams are "stacked" (their words, not mine) with really good students and some teams are forced to struggle with "lesser" students. This is a more difficult question to address. In talking with colleagues whom I consider to be excellent teachers, I have gotten a wide spectrum of advice on this point. One colleague stated that he historically put one team together made up of the poorest performers. He thought it served as a motivator and put them into a "make-or-break" mode. He claimed some dramatic success with this strategy. Other colleagues advocate distributing higher performing students among the teams.

A related problem is one of disciplinary diversity. Some students have been concerned that teams with more or fewer architects and/or construction managers (I have heard both sides of this argument) have an inherent advantage in this type of project format. I don't have much of a sense on this issue, which, by itself, is a good reason for more investigation.

Another change I have made involves using teams within the lecture portion of the course. I created a seating chart for the classroom lecture hall (not an easy task since it was in a theater-style classroom) and had the teams sit together during class. In addition, I created a series of activities for each lecture where each team had to select the best possible answer from a series of solutions. Most of the problems were such that a number of answers could be considered correct, depending on your perspective of the problem. We then debated the answers as a large group. I think this process has a great deal of potential, but it needs further investigation as well.

COMMENTARY 7.4

Tim illustrates the variety of issues he has previously considered when organizing student teams, the in-class efforts he has used to support teams, and possible factors that he hasn't fully explored.

INQUIRY HYPOTHESIS

Certainly, there are some facets of team structure that are fairly well known. Others are based on "common knowledge" which may or may not be accurate. For example, I know that teams that are too large are not functional in that some students then get "lost" and don't fully participate. I also know that teams that are too small don't have the resources necessary to fully develop a solution for the project. What I don't know and need to investigate are the following:

- What is the most effective team size for this course format?
- To what extent does the disciplinary diversity of the team enhance the learning environment?

These two questions can be linked into a single inquiry: *Is there an ideal team size and composition that enhances learning in my course?* This question is critical to the success of the course inasmuch as the course relies so heavily on team-based learning. From this question, I can develop my hypothesis: *There is an ideal size and composition of teams that will enhance learning in a course that utilizes service-learning semester projects.*

COMMENTARY 7.5

Tim first poses two questions, combines these into one overarching question, and then converts his question into a hypothesis statement. As there are often multiple paths to get to a destination, you too might follow a similar process as you define your classroom hypothesis.

INVESTIGATIVE PLAN

Since the primary goal of my course is to empower students to apply the fundamentals of mechanical systems, each team is required to submit a complete proposal in response to a Request for Proposal (RFP). The RFP is generated by the client (owner) of the building (for the service-learning project) and defines the recommendations that the client expects to receive relative to their building. It should also be noted that, as in my industry, there is no such thing as a correct answer. In general, there is a pool of right answers and my students must determine the best possible answer given their interpretation of the client's needs, recommendations, and requirements.

The challenge in proving my hypothesis is that the level of learning among students in a team is influenced by a number of variables, many of which may have no bearing at all on the team structure. The question that then arises is: *Can the other variables be kept constant so that I can accurately gauge the effect that team structure criteria have on learning?* If not, I might end up measuring something besides the effectiveness of the team. In carefully considering all the possible dependent variables for my hypothesis, I decided to limit my classroom inquiry to the following team structure variables:

- Team size
- The Architect/Construction Manager ratio for each team

Using the recitation session in which a student was enrolled as a starting point, I created student teams of different sizes and ratios of architects to construction managers. I ended up with 18 different student teams (five 6-person teams, five 5-person teams, and eight 4-person teams). The independent variables I used to measure my hypothesis were:

- Team grade on the written proposal
- Team grade on the drawdel

- The overall team grade on the service-learning project
- The students' perspectives of their learning and of their teammates' contributions

Some definitions will be helpful. A drawdel, by definition, is half drawing and half model. An example of a drawdel produced in this course is shown in Exhibit 7.2. Architects are typically more comfortable with this project component, as they are required in a number of their courses and are generally used, in one form or another, in industry. Construction managers, on the other hand, are generally more comfortable with the written proposal. A proposal written in response to an RFP is the most common method of acquiring projects in industry. My rubrics for evaluating the drawdel and the written report are presented in Exhibits 7.3 and 7.4.

Exhibit 7.2
Sample Student Drawdel

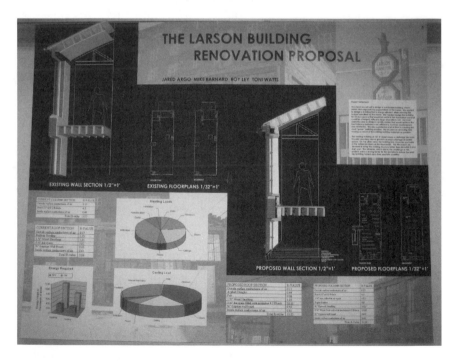

EXHIBIT 7.3
Rubric for Evaluating a Drawdel

Craft
- The drawdel should display a high level of craft comparable to a studio model.
- The drawdel should be integrated into the overall presentation board.
- The presentation board should be well designed.

Legibility
- The presentation board should be easy to read and understand.
- Components of the board (graphics, text, etc.) should be well organized.
- All components' relevance to the project should be explained.
- All graphs, pertinent images, and elements should be clearly labeled.

Clarity of Design
- The presentation board should sell your design and explain the reason for the design.
- Methods of presentation (plans, sections, etc.) should be legible and show evidence of a functional design.

Identification of Audience
- The presentation board should be geared toward the owner and work to gain their interest.
- Information on the board should be relevant.
- Calculations and numbers should only be used if they are understandable or explained.

EXHIBIT 7.4
Rubric for Evaluating a Written Report

- Clear expression of thought
- Depth of coverage (covers all aspects of course)
- LEED Energy Rating analysis and heating/cooling loads
- Reasonableness of cost/benefit ratio
- Meets the needs of the owner (constructability, etc.)
- Creativity and imagination
- Grammar, neatness, and professionalism

COMMENTARY 7.6

Tim provides a lot of useful information—definition of terms, identification of dependent variables (those that he is going to control), list of independent variables (data he is going to collect), and a discussion of their relevance. His rubrics for evaluating the team projects illustrate how he articulates criteria for student work. Notice that Tim's use of an actual photograph of a drawdel clarifies to readers what his students are creating.

INTERPRETING AND EVALUATING FINDINGS

Exhibit 7.5 summarizes the key results for the team-based project. As can be seen from the data, the four-person teams were less successful than the six- or five-person teams. The six-person teams performed the best overall, followed by the five-person teams. Interestingly, the six-person teams performed best on the written report, while the five-person teams performed best on the drawdel. The four-person teams lagged behind the performance of both the five-person and six-person teams for both the written report and the drawdel.

EXHIBIT 7.5
Team Results for the Service-Learning Project

Team Format	Arch/ CM	Report Grade	Drawdel Grade	Total Project Grade	Number of Underperformers
SIX-PERSON TEAMS					
Team A	3/3	89.7%	92.1%	90.3%	0
Team B	3/3	97%	89.8%	95.2%	2
Team C	3/2	90%	98.3%	92.1%	1
Team D	3/3	91.6%	92.6%	91.8%	2
Team E	3/3	90.6%	83.7%	88.9%	0
Average (six-person)		91.8%	91.3%	91.7%	*1*

Team Format	Arch/ CM	Report Grade	Drawdel Grade	Total Project Grade	Number of Underperformers
	FIVE-PERSON TEAMS				
Team F	2/3	89.3%	91.8%	89.9%	1
Team G	3/2	85.9%	94.7%	88.1%	1
Team H	2/3	92.7%	95.9%	93.5%	1
Team I	3/2	91.1%	89.4%	90.7%	1
Team J	2/3	90.7%	94.3%	91.6%	0
Average (five-person)		89.9%	93.2%	90.8%	0.8
	FOUR-PERSON TEAMS				
Team K	3/1	90.7%	89.8%	90.5%	1
Team L	2/2	82.6%	91.3%	84.8%	1
Team M	3/1	89.7%	95.9%	91.3%	1
Team N	2/2	91%	89.1%	90.5%	2
Team O	2/2	85.9%	90.4%	87%	1
Team P	2/2	88.1%	88%	88.1%	0
Team Q	1/3	92.2%	87.5%	91%	1
Team R	1/3	90.7%	93.1%	91.3%	1
Average (four-person)		89.6%	89.6%	89.6%	1

I also attempted to measure the number of "underperformers" found within each team. To measure this, I analyzed the students' assessments of their contributions and that of their fellow team members. The peer evaluation questions (Exhibit 7.6) required students to evaluate their own contribution (using a scale of 1 to 5) and the work of each team member (using a scale of 1 to 5). If a student's overall grade was significantly lowered by their fellow team members, I considered that person an underperformer for the purpose of this study. My concern with identifying underperformers was to test the long-held belief that you shouldn't make a team too large because inevitably a student will get "lost" and not learn at the same rate as the other students. On the surface, the number of underperformers seems consistent from team to team, regardless of team size, although the five-person teams had a slightly lower average of underperformers.

Exhibit 7.6
Students' Evaluation of Their and Their Teammates' Performance

Self-Evaluation of Own Performance
- I performed my share of the team's work.
- I provided relevant and timely information and research to the topic under study.
- I was cooperative and worked with the group to reach common goals.

Evaluation of Each Team Partner
- This partner performed their share of the team's work.
- This partner provided relevant and timely information and research to the topics under study.
- This partner was cooperative and worked with the group to reach common goals.

The data, I believe, take on a new perspective when the number of underperformers is compared to the Architect/Construction Manager ratio. Three observations become apparent. First, all the five-person teams had a fairly even Architect/Construction Manager ratio and they also had the lowest number average of underperformers. Second, all the teams that had no underperformers had perfectly balanced teams (i.e., the same number of architects to construction managers). Finally, the data show that all of the teams that had only one architect or one construction manager also had an underperformer. Once I dug further into the data, in 100% of the instances the underperformer was the architect or construction manager that was in the minority.

COMMENTARY 7.7

Tim's findings regarding the relationship between underperformers and "minority" status raises further questions he can cycle back into his teaching. Since student teams consistently identified the one team member who represented the "other" industry perspective as underperforming, this finding could be presented to students in subsequent course offerings and posed as an issue to explore. *Is it really true that the student is underperforming or is the student's different perspective viewed as a problem rather than as a resource to be valued?* Fostering such discussions might better prepare architecture and construction management students to interact with one another.

In reviewing the written comments from the anonymous student course evaluations, individuals (who were obviously from a four-person team) complained that they weren't as competitive as their colleagues in larger teams. The reason usually given was that the larger teams had a better opportunity to spread the workload and, therefore, could do more research, spend more time on the drawdel, and so on. This "noncompetitive" theme was found in a number of the student comments. The exact same point was made by several of the four-person teams during their exit critique with me after the semester project was turned in for grading. Those issues notwithstanding, these same students gave the course very high evaluations in terms of what they thought they learned and the format in which the learning took place. The overall high evaluations from both architecture and construction management students seem to indicate that the team-based learning approach, revolving around a real-life service-learning project, resonates among the students. Many students commented that they particularly liked the fact that they were being asked to perform in the classroom in exactly the same manner that they will be expected to perform in industry.

COMMENTARY 7.8

Tim does a good job of sharing his data and explaining his inquiry results. Given Tim's excellent record in teaching this course, we have no doubt about the positive student ratings or comments that he received about his course, but his discussion would be better supported if he included a summary (numerical or graphical) of the students' responses to key questions. Additionally, his approach for having students evaluate themselves and their teammates could be enhanced by having students write a reflection on what they accomplished and what each of their teammates accomplished.

> Possible questions include:
>
> • *What was the most significant contribution you made to the project?*
> • *What significant challenges did you face in completing this project?*
> • *What role did each of your team members bring to the project?*
>
> If Tim used such questions, his students' responses might offer more insight into the team dynamics and the sharing of responsibility for individual components of the project.

FINAL REFLECTION

A key outcome of my results casts some doubt on the wisdom of forming teams with only one member from a discipline present. The reason for my cross-linked course is to force the architects and construction managers to interact, as they will when they enter the workforce. My preliminary inquiry results seem to indicate that the poor relationships may be precipitated in environments that are unbalanced or unequal.

In reviewing my inquiry data, it is clear that more data needs to be kept on future courses to see if the trends uncovered in this effort reappear over time. However, for next year's class, I have already decided to make the following changes:

• Rely more on five- and six-person teams and less on four-person teams.
• Avoid teams with only a single discipline present.
• Create seven- and eight-person teams to see if there is an upper limit on team effectiveness.

Undoubtedly, there will be some other, smaller changes made as my course continues to evolve. The data seem to support my hypothesis that there is an optimal team size, although I don't think that the data collected to date answers the question just yet. In my opinion, the data seem to indicate that the optimal team size is probably within a range and that the range is higher than I anticipated when I started this process.

> ## COMMENTARY 7.9
>
> As Tim discusses, his inquiry is not done. He has preliminary data that suggest he is on the right track, but his project has made him

realize that he needs more information to be able to draw significant conclusions. The same might be true of your own inquiry project: It may stretch over two or more offerings of the course. And like Tim, you might find that becoming a scholarly teacher leads to continual improvement of your course that is reflected in greater student satisfaction and improved student learning.

POSTSCRIPT

In the subsequent term, the service-learning project for Tim's course focused around renovating a church built in 1907 into a community facility. Due to the project size, and the fact that it involved completely changing the function of the building, the project was probably the most ambitious he had ever attempted. Additionally, the owners of the building, as represented by their board of directors, were by far the most active and involved owners he had worked with. Their enthusiasm and involvement carried over to the students, influencing the student course evaluations, which were significantly more favorable than the previous year.

As planned, Tim changed the team size distribution to include teams of five, six, seven, and eight students. He found that the eight-person teams underperformed in comparison to teams of five, six, and seven. Although the six-person teams performed slightly better than the five- and seven-person teams, Tim did not find the difference to be statistically significant. More research on this point is necessary. All teams had at least two members of the same discipline, which reduced the possibility that the underperformance was due to a different perspective and not actual performance. As he predicted, Tim found that the number of underperformers appeared to be directly related to team size.

As Tim continues his inquiry into a third term, he is planning another service-learning project. He plans to structure the course to include teams of five, six, and seven students in order to continue testing his hypothesis that there is an ideal team size. In addition, Tim plans to examine whether team performance is correlated with grade point average of team members for certain disciplinary-based "fundamental" courses, which will help him determine whether team performance is related to the academic backgrounds of the team members.

CHAPTER EIGHT

USING CLASSROOM INQUIRY TO EVALUATE NEW ASSESSMENT MEASURES

Creating a class environment where the professor provides students with clearly defined goals, reasonable expectations, the tools that promote success, and reward for the hard work needed for the rigorous pursuit of intellect, knowledge, and critical thinking can only benefit the student and the professor.

—THOMAS BERG

INQUIRY OVERVIEW: Thomas explores the impact of having his students grade each other's essay examinations in his large first-year general education survey course of American history.

HIGHLIGHTS: Thomas shows how classroom inquiry can be a valuable tool for examining the effectiveness of different assessment measures. His course is a general education course and involves a large class size, both factors that influence his inquiry. His results yield significant information about the effectiveness of a new pedagogical approach and show him how he might refine that approach further if he decides to continue using it.

COURSE ACTIVITIES USED TO MEASURE INQUIRY QUESTION: Examination; student peer critique and review; student course evaluation; comparison of final grades to previous term.

INQUIRY PRESENTATION INCLUDES: Self-reflection; student commentary; bar chart; example of student essay.

ABOUT THE COURSE

My course, American History Since 1877, is a traditional one-semester general survey of the second half of American history. Exhibit 8.1 shares details of my course. No outside discussion or recitation sections supplement the three weekly lectures. Since my course is a survey, I must recognize that few of my students will aspire to be professional historians. However, as this course is usually the first introduction to higher levels of history, many students base their decision to major or minor in history on the quality of the teacher and the course as a whole. Encouraging students to enjoy history at the collegiate level and as a lifelong pleasure is one of my course goals. Most of my students face new challenges in my course. Many have never written essay examinations or long research papers. Their note-taking skills may not yet be ready for my fast-paced lecture environment. Moreover, the time management abilities of my first-year students are constantly challenged by an almost withering input of diverse and exciting opportunities; sometimes moving from building to building to attend classes is a challenge in itself. For these reasons, other course goals for my students include learning how to write more effective examinations and papers, learning better study habits, and perhaps even developing better time management skills.

Exhibit 8.1

Details of Thomas's Course

Discipline	History
Course	American History Since 1877
Course Level	First-year
Number of Students	268 (two sections of the course: 139 students in Section A and 129 students in Section B)
Type of Course	Large lecture course taken primarily to fulfill general education requirements
Meeting Time	Three days a week for 50 minutes
Grading Assistance	One graduate teaching assistant is responsible for grading the work of students in Section B

COMMENTARY 8.1

As we will see, Thomas's use of a large general education course for his classroom inquiry will provide some opportunities and some unique challenges. The fact that he is teaching two different sections of the same course gives him an opportunity to make comparisons between two groups of students, but his inquiry is complicated by the fact that he is working with a graduate teaching assistant who does the grading for one of the sections.

DEVELOPMENT OF THE INQUIRY

Written essay examinations help a student put together a narrative to answer a question, capitalizing on the mastery of detail and the ability to see the big picture. At the very least, an essay provides minimal practice of writing techniques and organization skills. I strongly believe in essay examinations because each student will use the skills repeatedly through life as they will answer most questions with detailed explanations, not bulleted outlines. Since many of my students have never written a collegiate-level essay examination, the task can be quite daunting. To maximize their potentials for writing, organization, and logic, I spend much effort in class on preparing them to write their essays as well and as comprehensively as possible.

PUTTING THE ISSUE INTO CONTEXT

For my classroom inquiry project, I have added in the requirement that each student must rate another student's essay examination, on the assumption that by being raters, they will become better essay writers themselves. Students learn from my grading of their examination; they can also learn much from personal observation and evaluation, given proper direction and a clearly defined methodology. Additionally, I envision that the synthesis of my "authoritative voice" with their rating will provide the students with another means of internalizing information, expose them to another writing style, increase their practice in writing mechanics, and allow them to take a leadership role in class by rating and suggesting a grade.

COMMENTARY 8.2

With 268 students in two sections of his course, the logistical issues involved in this classroom inquiry are daunting. Not only does Thomas need to develop a plan for having his students rate each other's work, but he also needs to collect data to document his inquiry. When carrying out inquiry projects focused on large classes, many teachers use sampling techniques that draw from a class subset.

INQUIRY HYPOTHESIS

My classroom inquiry explores the following hypothesis: *Upon receiving adequate instruction, examples of good, average, and poor work, and some practice, my students should be able to critique accurately another student's essay examination to within half a letter grade (± 5 points on a 100-point scale) of my standard.* My "dream goal" is to have a student rater's grade be within ±3 points of my assigned grade. I also wonder if the new examination technique will reduce the time that I spend grading each examination, since student rater comments will already highlight most of the issues in an essay. Finally, I do realize that my grading standards may differ from those of other teachers, but this poses another learning opportunity for students to practice flexibility in their work and performances since no two professors, jobs, or situations are exactly alike.

COMMENTARY 8.3

While Thomas sets a quantifiable standard for measuring his results, he does not specify what percentage of his students should achieve this standard. *Should 100% of the student ratings be ± 5 points, or is it sufficient if 90% reach this goal?* In acknowledging that his grading standards could differ from those of others, he offers a potential limitation of his inquiry. This should not be an issue in Thomas's case, since he is trying to help his students achieve his grading standards, not some "universal" standard for rating essay exams. It is important to define and share any potential limitations you might be aware of as you develop your own classroom inquiry. Beyond the value of having students better understand and use his criteria for good essay writing, Thomas hypothesizes that this project might also benefit him by reducing his grading time. Incorporating peer comments into the assessment process may indeed make the grading process easier and faster—a significant consideration in a class of this size.

INVESTIGATIVE PLAN

I used the new examination technique in two sections (Section A and Section B) of my course taught in the same term. In both course sections, each student either wrote the first examination and "rated" the second examination or vice versa, while all students were required to write the final noncomprehensive examination. (I use the words *rater* and *rating* to distinguish the students' work from mine as I am ultimately responsible for assigning the official grade to their examinations.) One week in advance of the examination, I gave the students three possible essay questions, from which I randomly selected one for the examination. All students had to study each question regardless of whether they wrote on or rated the exam. I also assigned the students special identification numbers, 1 through X (the latter being the total number of students in the class section), so that no student's name would appear on the examination blue book. The class period before the examination, I held a type of lottery in which five students randomly drew from a hat the numbers 0 through 9 to determine which 50% of the students would write the examination; the other 50% automatically rated the examination. The numbers drawn corresponded to the last digits of the students' special identification numbers. With this drawing, students could then plan on either writing or rating the second examination, knowing that every student would write the third examination.

On examination day, 50% of the students wrote the essay in a blue book, using carbon paper to create a copy onto blank white paper. Students were also required to write their essay on every other line of the blue book, allowing for easier reading, rating, and grading. At the next class session after the examination, after discussing my grading criteria with the other 50% of my students, I distributed the carbon copies of the examinations and purple ink pens (in contrast to the red ink pens that I use) with which they were to write comments. I used nearly $60 of my own money to purchase the pens and carbon paper. Using the class identification number, I also recorded which student was rating which examination. Students were to write comments and observations throughout the examination, give an overall percentage and letter grade, and return the carbon copy examination at the next class period. Following their return, I (or my teaching assistant) evaluated both the written essay and the rater's comments, correcting each as needed, and assigning a final grade on the essay. We reserved the right to determine the final grade, but took into account the rater's comments and proposed grade.

COMMENTARY 8.4

As a means of managing a large number of students, Thomas put in place some useful and detailed examination policies. Before distributing the essays for his students to critique, Thomas described the grading criteria for that essay with the students so that they would know what specifically to look for as they rated it. A good rule of thumb when describing your inquiry procedure is to provide all the information that readers would need to carry out the inquiry themselves. Also note that Thomas spent his own money to purchase the materials needed for the inquiry. He might have asked his department to purchase these supplies, but sometimes the resources are not available or you don't realize that you will need them until the last minute. In planning your own inquiry project, be sure to consider whether you will need any additional resources and how you might obtain them.

I taught both sections of the course, but I graded Section A's examinations, while my teaching assistant graded Section B's examinations. While I explained my new examination procedures and my expectations regarding students' performance to my teaching assistant, we did not discuss the progress of the classroom inquiry during the semester. Instead, I gave him carte blanche in how he graded, provided he followed my general direction and grading philosophy that the average student should be able to write at a B level, or 84% to 85%.

COMMENTARY 8.5

The size of Thomas's classes makes it necessary to have a teaching assistant to help with the grading, which raises questions of comparability between the two sections. Thomas takes advantage of this to create a "control" group to compare with the section whose exams he grades himself. As you will see, the results of this comparison raise more questions for Thomas. To limit the variation between the two sections, it might have been useful if Thomas established more formal grading rubrics for both his graduate assistant and his students to use in rating the exams.

INTERPRETING AND EVALUATING FINDINGS

The differences between the results for Section A and Section B of my course are akin to a Dr. Jekyll and Mr. Hyde scenario, and I am wondering how to explain the severe differences. Remember, my goal was to have student raters assign grades within ± 5 points of my (and my teaching assistant's) assessments. Exhibit 8.2 shows the discrepancy of the grades between what I assigned and what the student raters assigned for the two examinations in Section A of my course. In the first examination, 7% of the student raters and I gave the same score (thus, 0-point difference); 14% gave a score of 1 to 3 points more than I did, while 23% gave a score of 1 to 3 points less; 4% gave a score of 4 to 5 points more, while 7% gave a score 4 to 5 points less than I did. Overall, I substantially increased 10% of the rated grades and substantially decreased 13%. (I defined *substantial* by increasing or decreasing a grade by 10 points, or a full letter grade.) My most significant corrections occurred because the rating student was either much too harsh or much too generous.

EXHIBIT 8.2
Discrepancy of Grades for Section A

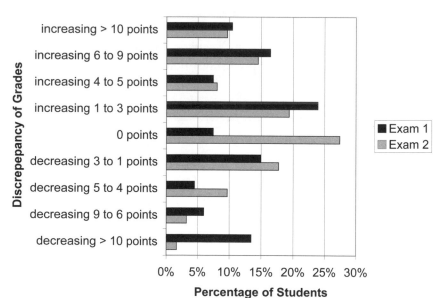

The average student rater's grade was 81.7% compared to my 83.0%, a difference of 1.3%. This surprised me because I thought that my students would grade an essay examination much harder due to their inexperience or more critical eye. On the whole, 58% of the student rater grades were within my ±5 standard and 44% were ±3 points from my "dream" standard. Exhibit 8.3 shows an example of a student rater's comments for an essay—the pro and con comments were written by the student rater and my remarks are at the bottom of the page along with my assigning the same grade as the student rater.

Exhibit 8.3
Example of Student Rater Comments

Student Comments:

Paper Grade: 82%. Here are some pros and cons about your paper

PROS:
- Spelling
- Punctuation
- Sentence structure
- A few good statements and facts
- Built off of these statements
- Answer most of the questions

CONS:
- Clarity
- Run-on sentences
- Need to list some dates to help reader understand the time frame
- Need to list some facts about who these people were and about how they lived
- Refocus the main ideas of progressivism
- Discuss the political success of the movement and research goals that took place before the war
- Progressive era's legacy for America, then and now?
- Leaders besides the Muckrakers

Tom's Comments:

Paper Grade: B- (82%)
Rater: Good work! All ratings should be this complete and conscientious; 20 out of 20

For the second examination, 25% of the student raters and I gave the same score; 16% gave scores of 1 to 3 points more than I did, while 17% gave scores of 1 to 3 points less than I did; 9% gave a score of 4 to 5 points more, while 7% gave a score 4 to 5 points less. Overall, I substantially increased 9% of the student-rated grades and substantially decreased only 1%. The average student rater's grade was 80.6% compared to my 82.4%, a difference of 1.8%. While the difference between the student rater average versus my average increased slightly, 82% of the rater grades were within my ±5 standard, and 65% were within ±3 points.

COMMENTARY 8.6

Thomas's use of a graph to present the examination results provides a clear and concise description of the outcomes. In addition, his inclusion of an example of a graded essay helps readers see the type of comments student raters made.

In comparing the two examinations for Section A, the data matches the way I assumed the experience would go. For the first examination, I thought that few students would exactly match my standard of grading, with some students being too generous and far more students being more critical than I. After the first examination, I discussed with my students their performance as writers and raters, identifying common errors, silly mistakes, and examples of good essays and what made them good. Due to time constraints, I was not able to return the graded examination for the student rater to inspect before returning it to the student author.

The results for the second examination closely resemble a typical bell curve: a traditional distribution of grades with a slight flair on the right. The students who gave tougher grades matched my initial prediction that students would grade more harshly than I did. Apparently, the raters of the first examination (authors of the second examination) learned how to write a better essay, and the authors of the first examination (raters of the second examination) learned how to rate an essay more effectively. Overall, I am encouraged to see that significantly more students were grading on my standard and that my "dream goal" seemed attainable.

The results for Section B of my course show a complete reversal of what was observed in Section A. Referring to Exhibit 8.4, in the first examination, 19% of the student raters gave the same score as my teaching assistant; 18% gave a score of 1 to 3 points more, while 36% gave a score of 1 to 3 points less; 7% gave a score of 4 to 5 points more, while 7% gave a score 4 to 5 points less than he did. My teaching assistant substantially increased 1% of the student rater grades and substantially decreased 1%. The average student rater's grade was 81.2% compared to my teaching assistant's 81.9%, a difference of 0.7%. On the whole, 88% of the rater grades were within ±5 points of his standard (73% within ±3).

EXHIBIT 8.4
Discrepancy of Grades for Section B

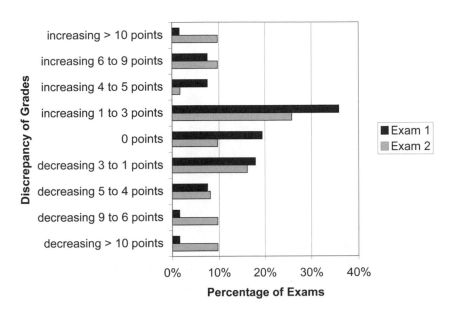

For the second examination, 10% of the student raters and my teaching assistant gave the same score; 16% gave scores of 1 to 3 points more than he did, while 26% gave a score of 1 to 3 points less; 8% gave scores of 4 to 5 points more, while 1% gave a score 4 to 5 points less than he did. My teaching assistant substantially increased 10% of the student rater's grades and substantially decreased 10%. The average rater's grade was 82.9% compared to his 83.2%, a difference of 0.3%. For this examination, 61% were within ±5 points of my teaching assistant's standard (52% within ±3 points).

The results for Section B's first examination more or less resemble a bell curve. I was surprised to see a close match between the raters' grades and those assigned by my teaching assistant, especially for a first examination. This pattern ran contrary to my original thoughts and to what I observed in Section A. The results for the second examination follow a much more distributed pattern. I would have expected this pattern for the first examination, but certainly not for the second.

Quite curiously, in Section A of the course, the second examination's grade distribution becomes more balanced, even though the difference in the student raters' and my averages increased. By comparison, in Section B the second examination's grade distribution became more unbalanced, even though the difference in the student raters' and my teaching assistant's averages grew closer. I believe that no single reason explains the discrepancy between Sections A and B, but a combination of reasons coalesced to create what appears to be havoc with the data.

COMMENTARY 8.7

Thomas was puzzled by the very different results from his two course sections, which drew his attention away from the fact that students in both sections did well in matching his ±5-point criteria. In fact, if his overall goal was to heighten students' awareness of the criteria used to grade their essays, then his inquiry succeeded. Because of the range of student backgrounds, abilities, and motivation in a general education course such as this one, it is unrealistic to expect 100% conformity to his grading standards. Since Thomas did not specify a defined measurable number of students (e.g., 50%, 75%) that he wanted to meet his grading criteria at the outset of his inquiry, it is hard for him to claim success or failure.

Adding to the confusion, it seems that two issues are being tracked here: 1) the differences between the teacher's and the students' ratings of the examinations, and 2) a comparison of the scores on both examinations. It is possible that the amount and level of knowledge being tested on each examination differed—perhaps the second examination was harder because there was more information to learn or it was more complex. It is more valuable for Thomas to focus on whether the teacher's and students' grades were the same, since this finding demonstrates that students understand the grading criteria, whether or not they can meet them.

To explain the discrepancies between the performances of Sections A and B, I have to consider several possibilities. First, as the person conducting the inquiry, I subconsciously could have attenuated my second examination grades to meet my expectations that the raters' grades would mirror more closely my standard given proper instruction and motivation. The question *Did I get what I wanted to see?* is of intense interest.

While I tried to ensure that my grading technique remained constant from the first to the second examinations, I cannot state that it remained absolutely so; I can only rely on my years of experience grading the same and similar questions to maintain a constant grading criteria.

Second, I may not have explained as adequately as possible my grading criteria to my teaching assistant. Perhaps with inadequate instruction from me, he tried to follow conscientiously the student rater's grade in the first examination, but then changed his manner or grading philosophy on the second examination; it's possible he "overworked" the essays and found discrepancies where none really existed. Somewhere during the classroom inquiry, I might have intuited the process without communicating to him my evolving ideas.

Third, perhaps student raters in Section B did not learn enough from me when I discussed the most common examination errors, shared examples of poor writing techniques, and discussed ways to improve the essays. Also, perhaps the students who rated the second examination were complacent in thinking that their rating of the first examination was adequate, because the teaching assistant did not vary much from their scores. As with Section A, I had intended to distribute the essays to the student raters for an "after action analysis," but did not due to time constraints.

I wish that I could make a direct connection between the students' writing and examination rating and their final course grade. Unfortunately, with such a limited base from which to extract information, I believe that any linkage would be forced and not directly supported by the data. To explore adequately the relationship with this new examination technique and the final course grade, students would need to rate and write far more examinations than just one. However, I am pleased with incremental change even if it is small, so long as the change is positive for the student.

COMMENTARY 8.8

Thomas's summary of potential confounding factors—his own grading, his directions to his teaching assistant, his students' complacency—present valid concerns and could all contribute to the differences between the two sections. The differences also could be caused by random chance or by something outside of his control. Since classroom inquiry projects involve people and are not done in a controlled laboratory environment, there is always the chance of uncontrolled factors influencing the results. The best strategy is to identify as many of the factors that you can control so as to minimize the impact of those you cannot control. In some inquiry projects, even the most detailed planning will not help.

The students in both Sections A and B improved their final examination grades by roughly 3%, which is comparable to previous classes. However, I cannot demonstrate conclusively that the new examination technique was critical to this improvement, since other students in previous terms using a traditional three-examination system had similar improvements. I believe that the new examination technique is useful for students, provided they receive adequate instruction in studying for, writing, and rating an essay examination.

COMMENTARY 8.9

While Thomas notes that his students' essay writing skills did improve on the final examination, he did not feel he had the data to make the connection between this improvement and the new examination technique. *Did the rating activity itself help or was the improvement due to the repeated experience of writing examinations in general?* Whatever the answer, many would argue that any attention to grading criteria will help students better understand what is expected of them. Overall, being able to draw a cause and effect result is difficult for many classroom inquiry projects. A primary goal for classroom inquiry is to improve student learning, not to perform a statistically pure inquiry. The key is to identify a well-defined question, create a good investigative plan, and control for as many factors as you can.

Just as the differences in the sections' performances surprised me, so did the responses garnered in the Department of History's mandatory, standardized student course evaluation. Students wrote their responses in the appropriate "What did you like about this course?" and "What would you change in this course?" questions. In Section A, 14 students specifically referred to or discussed the new examination technique. Of these respondents, 10 students made positive comments, while 4 students were decidedly negative. In Section B, 16 students specifically referred to or discussed the new examination technique; 13 students made positive statements, while 3 students were decidedly negative. Exhibit 8.5 shares some of the comments from students.

Exhibit 8.5
Student Comments About the Examinations

Some Positive Comments
- "I liked having the opportunity to rate the second exam."
- "I liked how he had us grade an exam & take an exam. It gives us a better perspective on learning to write and memorize facts."
- "I liked the rate & write part of the exams I thought that was cool."
- "Good method for exams."
- "I loved being able to grade someone else's essay then also see what they gave me w/ responses."
- "I liked grading the exams. I learned a lot from grading on how to improve my essays the next time. Maybe give more tests."
- "Like alternating writing & rating."
- "Exam method was good."
- "I liked how we got to see what others thought of our essays—gave us a chance to see good writing & horrible writing."
- "I liked the rating/writing system."

Some Negative Comments
- "Whole 'rate student's exam' isn't that great."
- "Having other students grade the exams wasn't the best idea."
- "I am not . . . comfortable w/ the rate & take stuff."
- "[Need a] less confusing way of testing."

In the weeks preceding the final examination, two students visited my office and said that they liked rating an essay. Given that students seldom visit my office, having two students specifically mention their rating experience without my prompting them is significant feedback. These students believed that rating another student's examination gave them more insight into how to write a better essay.

COMMENTARY 8.10

Thomas did not initially plan to include student perceptions as one of the ways to evaluate the effectiveness of his new grading method. But the responses on the student evaluations and discussions with students persuaded him that this was an important factor to consider. If he chooses to use this technique again, he might plan to obtain more direct input from all students by means of a formal survey, possibly administered and collected by his teaching assistant and held until after final grades are turned in. Or he could develop a survey to be administered by a web-based academic portal (e.g., Blackboard, WebCT).

Thomas was reassured when two students commented on how much they liked the examination practice. In Chapter 1, we remarked that we as teachers often "grasp" at any informal feedback and assume this is true for all students. In Thomas's case, the student comments helped confirm the value of his classroom inquiry. *What if his students had said that they did not like it? Would this have been enough to discourage him from applying this approach again?* If he had not followed a more formal inquiry procedure, he would have no other information on which to base his evaluation of the technique's usefulness.

FINAL REFLECTION

Grading the examinations did not take me less time as I had hypothesized (and hoped); in fact, the opposite was true. Because it required more grading time, this examination technique would work better for classes no larger than 30 (assuming 15 minutes total to grade the essay and evaluate the rating comments, which I discovered to be my pace). I would use this same examination technique for a general survey Honors class (with a limited enrollment) or an upper-division class in which the prerequisite knowledge of American history is stronger and students' ability to draw on it is better. I would also increase the opportunities to rate an examination from only once to as much as three times, even though this might require one more class period used for an examination. Though if adding a third examination during the term, perhaps I can make it a take-home examination that counts for slightly less than the other two examinations.

I don't know if I will use the same laborious examination technique again for my large general survey course. Instead, I might offer a "practice question" that provides students with nearly the same opportunity for critique, but I would need to work out how to fit this into the course curriculum. Additionally, I should devote more time to grading examples of students' essay questions before their eyes (using an electronic document reader), so they will better understand my theory of grading and learn how to write better. Also, I might consider using this technique only for students who wish to receive an A in any particular class in which I use a "contract system" for grades, the policies of which I am still exploring.

COMMENTARY 8.11

Thomas's inquiry yielded results that are quite common whenever we introduce a new assessment technique or pedagogical method: The outcome was somewhat favorable, but not as clearly positive as he would have liked. This response highlights a problem we all face: *Are we willing to take risks in our courses by experimenting with the way we teach, and if so, how long does it take to refine a new teaching method before it is as effective as we had hoped it would be?* Because Thomas concluded that his new grading technique did not work well in a large class, it might be easy to see the inquiry as a "failure," but in fact it yielded some important evidence and raises new questions about student learning. The results from Section A confirmed his hypothesis that students do learn from having to rate/critique the work of others, while student comments indicated that many of them valued having this opportunity. The results from Section B suggest that perhaps he needs to work more closely with his teaching assistant in developing more structured grading rubrics. And while Thomas may be hesitant to use this grading technique for the "high stakes" of essay examinations, he is considering other ways that critique might be incorporated into his daily curriculum. Indeed, Thomas may find that repeated exposure to critiques on a smaller scale might reap similar student benefits while it reduces his time spent grading. The inquiry as a whole has caused Thomas to think about other related ways to help students improve their essay-writing skills. All of these issues point to new "problems" in Randy Bass's (1999) sense of the word: questions that generate further inquiry into student learning.

CHAPTER NINE

CLASSROOM INQUIRY FOR MEASURING FEEDBACK ON STUDENT LEARNING AND APTITUDES

The results of my classroom inquiry were so encouraging that they moti-vated me to completely change my instructional approach. As a result of my increased awareness of my students' learning, I have made the leap to a 100% student-centered pedagogy.

—KEVIN LEE

INQUIRY OVERVIEW: Kevin examines the effect of web-based assessment practices on his students' performance and attitudes in his first-year astronomy course.

HIGHLIGHTS: Kevin uses his inquiry to examine the effectiveness of several different assessment measures in a large general education course. He uses a variety of data collection methods that yield interesting results. Kevin's inquiry directly addresses many of the difficulties faced by those who teach large general education survey courses, including tremendous variation in student background and preparedness and student preconceptions about course content. Because it considers so many issues, Kevin's inquiry is a complex and well-documented description of his teaching that caused him to rethink his approach to teaching this course.

COURSE ACTIVITIES USED TO MEASURE INQUIRY QUESTION: Homework/assignment; quiz; examination; pre- and post-assessment; survey of student opinions; disciplinary-based diagnostic test; comparison of final grades to previous term.

INQUIRY PRESENTATION INCLUDES: Self-reflection; data table; example of homework question; example of examination question; copy of student survey; excerpts from course syllabus.

ABOUT THE COURSE

My course, Descriptive Astronomy, is a general education science course that is typically taken by first-year students. Exhibit 9.1 shares details of my course. During any given year, more than 1,400 students at my school take this course. For the vast majority, this course is the only one taken from my department (physics and astronomy). The students' widely varied backgrounds present a major obstacle in teaching the course. A few students find the course simplistic, while many others find it overly difficult. Students also often enter the course with erroneous expectations of what astronomy is all about. They expect to learn the names of planets, stars, and constellations and to be able to tell mythological stories about them. When they discover that they are in a true *science* course and are expected to understand concepts such as the energy levels of the hydrogen atom and nuclear binding energy, they are often disappointed and frustrated. In general, this student response is common across the nation; students start out liking astronomy and leave the course not liking it as much.

Exhibit 9.1

Details of Kevin's Course

Discipline	Astronomy
Course	Descriptive Astronomy
Course Level	First-year
Number of Students	148
Type of Course	A general education science course that attracts a diverse mixture of students
Meeting Time	Three 50-minute class sessions per week

Exhibit 9.2 summarizes the specific goals I have for the course. My course also reinforces several useful skills beyond knowledge of astronomy. For instance, students are asked to use basic mathematical reasoning such as linear proportionality for extracting information from a variety of graphs and diagrams. Higher reasoning also is used in the course, especially spatial reasoning, which will be useful to them throughout their lives. I hope that once students complete this course, they are able to read a newspaper article about astronomy and understand it. Additionally, when they go outside and look up at the sky, they should understand from a scientific standpoint what they see and why it is there.

EXHIBIT 9.2
Summary of the Goals for Kevin's Course

Goal: Students should leave this course with an understanding of what they see in the sky.

1. What is the path of the sun across the sky and how does that path vary with latitude and time of year and give rise to seasons on the earth?
2. Where can the moon and planets be found in the sky, how do they appear and move relative to the background stars, and how is that a function of latitude on the earth?
3. What are the shapes of star trails in the sky, and how do they vary with latitude and direction of view?

These are the types of astronomical phenomena that students regularly see in the night sky. Understanding the appearance of the sky is important because everyone should have a basic understanding of their surroundings.

Goal: Students should gain a sense of perspective in regard to space and time.

1. The universe has been around for about 12 billion years.
2. We can see objects with the Hubble Space Telescope that are so far away it has taken 10 billion years for their light to get to us.
3. Our sun is one of about 100 billion stars in the Milky Way Galaxy, which is one of about 100 billion galaxies in the universe.

All of these statements illustrate the enormous scales of space and time that are discussed in astronomy classes. These scales dwarf the size of our planet and the length of recorded human history. These comparisons are important to help students understand how peripheral human beings are in the universe.

Goal: Students should understand the scientific method.

I summarize the scientific method as observe, theorize, and verify. Students need to know that science is a continual process of checking and rechecking knowledge, and nothing is accepted on faith. I also stress the importance of observing in an unbiased manner.

COMMENTARY 9.1

Kevin begins his inquiry by outlining his course goals and describing what he wants students to be able to learn by the end of the semester. This description helps readers develop a clear picture of the course and to understand the significance of his inquiry hypothesis. Unlike some of the pre-professional courses profiled in previous chapters, Kevin's course is designed to introduce basic scientific principles to students who probably won't be future scientists. As such, it could be classified as a general education course designed to teach students how to understand the role of science in their daily lives. These courses are often challenging to teach, particularly because they attract a diverse range of students.

DEVELOPMENT OF THE INQUIRY

As part of the design of my course, I make use of EDU, an extremely flexible and powerful Internet-based assessment tool. Unlike more familiar web-based academic portals (e.g., Blackboard, WebCT), EDU focuses entirely on assessment. It allows teachers to develop online assessment instruments for testing students on their learning—for example, by incorporating images, tables of data, animations, and many other resources into assessment questions. It also has numerous question randomization capabilities, and it automatically grades student work and records those grades.

In my course, students interact with EDU in three ways during the semester. Before every class, students must complete a brief EDU reading quiz on the material to be covered that day. While I repeat the key reading points during class, this method allows the presentation of basic information to be very brief and leaves more time for classroom activities. I have observed that students learn more from each lecture, since they have a foundation on which to put my presentation into context. Each reading quiz typically contains a few multiple-choice questions on the main reading concepts and takes about 10 minutes to complete. Students can take the quiz as many times as they want in the 24 hours prior to class. Since I have a large test bank of questions and I employ the randomization feature within EDU, students will not get the same questions on each attempt.

Students also must complete an online homework assignment that covers approximately a week's worth of course material. A homework assignment consists of 10 to 18 randomly selected questions. As with the quizzes, students can redo this assignment as many times as they want during the one-week period with only the highest grade counting.

Finally, there are four examinations for the course. The examinations are closed-book and notes, and students must complete them within one hour (two hours for the final examination). All of these examinations are in a multiple-choice question format and are taken on a computer using the EDU system. Students have a one-week window in which to complete each examination. A student is allowed two practice attempts (which are not graded) prior to their "graded" attempt. The "graded" attempt (the only one that counts toward their grade) is proctored and administered in a computer-based testing center.

By allowing my students to retake quizzes and homework and to take practice examinations, I have designed the course so that if students put in the time and effort to learn, they should do well.

COMMENTARY 9.2

Kevin's philosophy of allowing students to redo work follows the model of "mastery learning," in which students practice repeatedly until they can demonstrate that they have mastered a topic. Using EDU for the assessment of mastery learning has both pros and cons. With 148 students in the course, it is a tremendous advantage to have the majority of the course grading done automatically by the computer. The drawback is that Kevin needs to create a very large test bank of questions so that students will not receive the same question when they retake the assessments. Once this test bank is developed, though, Kevin can use it in successive course offerings.

PUTTING THE ISSUE INTO CONTEXT

Many studies have shown that no variable correlates better with academic success than time on task. Thus, it is very important that students be willing and able to spend a sufficient amount of time to learn the material. This student commitment is especially important in an introductory science course where most students are challenged by the subject matter and the large amount of course material to be covered. I believe that my use of EDU and of mastery learning techniques have helped, although I am uncertain of their actual impact on my students.

INQUIRY HYPOTHESIS

My classroom inquiry will explore the question: *What is the effect of my Internet-based testing on student performance and attitudes?*

COMMENTARY 9.3

As you will soon see, Kevin uses different approaches for answering this question. The first area he will focus on is the impact of EDU on student performance in his course. The second area will examine whether EDU improves his students' attitudes toward astronomy.

INVESTIGATIVE PLAN

Several different criteria will be used to evaluate student learning, experiences, and attitudes in this course. To measure student use of the EDU system, I will look at statistics on student usage. I will then explore the impact of EDU's usage on their grades. To collect students' perceptions, I will sample their thoughts on EDU's impact. To measure their changes in attitude toward astronomy, I will compare the results of a pretest/post-test that I administered to the students. Finally, I will use a nationally developed astronomy diagnostic survey to compare my students' learning to national norms.

COMMENTARY 9.4

It may seem that Kevin plans to collect an overwhelming amount of data, but his plan can be carried out fairly easily. The EDU usage statistics will be collected automatically by the computer. Kevin will also administer two surveys, the first on EDU usage and the second to diagnose astronomy learning. Finally, he will give his students a pre- and post-test to measure their attitudes toward astronomy. These surveys should provide him with a well-rounded sense of how EDU functions in promoting student learning and changing student attitudes in his class.

INTERPRETING AND EVALUATING FINDINGS

Students completed a reading quiz before each class except when a homework assignment was due on that day. This amounted to 32 reading quizzes (consisting of three to five questions) during the term. Exhibit 9.3 gives an example of the type of questions asked. An analysis of the EDU statistics showed that the 32 quizzes were taken a total of 9,389 times. On average, each student made a total of 63 attempts (with a standard deviation of 28) for the 32 quizzes—in other words, they took each quiz two times. The large standard deviation shows high variation in the number of attempts, with some students taking each quiz more than twice and some taking it only once.

Exhibit 9.3

Example Questions From a Reading Quiz

Question 1: Nuclear reactions occur in the sun's
 (a) Photosphere
 (b) Chromosphere
 (c) Corona
 (d) Convective zone
 (e) Core

Question 2: The process whereby energy is released from combining small nuclei into larger ones is called
 (a) Fusion
 (b) Fission
 (c) Binding energy
 (d) Convection
 (e) Conduction

Question 3: In the formula $E = mc^2$, the letter c stands for
 (a) The speed of sound
 (b) The speed of an electron around the nucleus
 (c) The amount of energy contained in one hydrogen nucleus
 (d) The energy of a neutrino emerging from the sun
 (e) The speed of light

During the term, students completed 14 EDU homework assignments (each consisting of about 12 questions). These questions were substantially more difficult than the reading quiz questions and often required students to extract information from maps and diagrams. The 14 homework assignments were taken a total of 9,192 times during the term. On average, each student attempted the 14 homework assignments 63 times (with a standard deviation of 41), or 4.5 attempts per student per homework assignment. Again, the high standard deviation shows that some students made lots of use of this retake feature and others did not. After the due date, the assignments were converted to a practice mode within EDU but remained available for students. Unfortunately, the EDU system did not record attempts in this mode. If it did, the average would be higher since I know many students went back and used the homework assignments as a means of studying for the examinations.

COMMENTARY 9.5

Here Kevin makes an important observation regarding the limits of EDU in recording students' usage in studying for the course examinations. Since the EDU system doesn't record this data, Kevin might consider asking a question on the post-survey regarding how students used EDU to study.

Each of the four examinations had a practice version within EDU that could be taken twice before students took the proctored version at the testing center. As described, EDU would not collect data while in the practice mode, so I don't have any numbers. Through conversations with students, I do know that many students routinely took advantage of this.

Overall, my students spent a significant amount of time using the EDU system. This system effectively provides a public test bank that encourages students to practice, build mastery, and get regular feedback regarding their progress before they are required to demonstrate expertise on a closed-book proctored examination. The averages cited earlier illustrate that many students took advantage of the system. However, the standard deviations indicate that the use varied considerably from one student to another.

COMMENTARY 9.6

The summary statistics provide a useful guide on how students used the EDU system. If Kevin had been able to obtain them, statistics from the practice sessions would be useful. Also, if EDU collected such information, it would be interesting to see some summary data concerning the average time students spent online using the assessments. A completely different inquiry question would be to explore at what times of the day/week students interacted with the EDU system and whether that influenced their classroom performance.

The final course grade point average was 2.62 (out of 4.00). However, this average was significantly lowered by a handful of students who received failing grades for the course. Overall, 35.9% of the students in the course received an A+, A, or A–. Twenty-four percent received some type of B. Around 30% of the students who started the course later withdrew or received a D or less. As such the results are very bimodal— students either did very well or very poorly. I have observed this pattern as EDU usage has increased, and it is much different from the results prior to EDU's usage. Then, the distribution of grades was more of a "flat" bell-shaped curve.

COMMENTARY 9.7

One of the disadvantages of using an average is that it is highly influenced by outliers within a dataset. Often it is helpful to report a median in addition to the average to allow one to see how the results might be skewed in one direction or the other. Kevin might also consider using graphs to illustrate the grade distribution for this course and/or to compare the grade distribution for this course with that from a previous offering.

When I linked the EDU usage data to individual student grades, I found a direct, positive correlation between the number of attempts for a reading quiz or a homework assignment and the student's final grade.

Exhibit 9.4 presents my analysis. A typical student who received an A in the course attempted the 32 reading quizzes more than 77 times and the 14 homework assignments more than 90 times. In comparison, a student who received a D attempted the reading quizzes around 57 times and the homework assignments 46 times. As I previously mentioned, I know this homework number is higher for the better-performing students since many used the homework to study for their examinations.

EXHIBIT 9.4

Relationship Between EDU Usage and Student's Final Grade

Grade	Final Course Percentage	Reading Quiz (average total number of attempts)	Homework Assignment (average total number of attempts)
A	Greater than 85%	77.6	90.3
B	Between 75% and 85%	73.8	69.1
C	Between 65% and 75%	66.8	70.5
D	Between 50% and 65%	57.4	46.1
F	Less than 50%	21.6	12.8

COMMENTARY 9.8

Kevin's results confirm his previous statement that time on task is the primary metric for determining academic success. He might find it useful to share these results with his students when he teaches the course again.

At the end of the term, 97 of my students completed a survey to determine how the EDU system influenced their learning. The survey used a 5-point scale (Strongly Agree = 5, Agree = 4, Neutral = 3, Disagree = 2, and Strongly Disagree = 1) as a response to each statement. Exhibit 9.5 displays the results. Students rated statements 1, 11, and 12 very highly, thus indicating a strong level of enthusiasm for EDU. The responses to Statement 9 show that students took advantage of the repeated attempts of quizzes and assignments without using their textbook or notes. This data demonstrate that students bought into the idea of building mastery through repeated practice. Most telling is the response to Statement 6, in which students indicated that the EDU system significantly improved their learning. Not surprisingly, the answer to Statement 4 shows that students were not overly enthused with the subject matter.

EXHIBIT 9.5

Results From Student Survey on EDU Usage

Statement	Average Student Response
1. I enjoyed using the EDU system.	4.1
2. I got discouraged by computer problems when using EDU.	2.3
3. I dislike trying to learn with computers.	2.0
4. I like the subject matter of the course.	3.2
5. The EDU system helped me to learn the material.	3.9
6. I would have learned just as much studying on my own.	2.2
7. EDU helped my grade in the course.	3.9
8. I often collaborated with other students when working on EDU assignments.	2.3
9. I often took EDU assignments without my textbook or notes to test my knowledge.	3.8
10. I didn't take full advantage of EDU.	2.6
11. I would retake assignments until I was happy with my grade.	4.4
12. I wish more of my classes would use EDU.	4.0

COMMENTARY 9.9

The answer to the first of Kevin's questions, whether EDU has a positive impact on student learning, is a resounding yes. The student survey clearly shows that students felt that they learned more using the EDU system and the mastery learning approach, while the grade distribution provides an objective measure of improved student learning that was directly linked to use of EDU. For this reason, the answer to Kevin's second question, whether EDU increases student interest in astronomy, may come as a surprise.

In an attempt to measure my students' attitude toward astronomy, I administered a pre- and post-test survey to my students. Developed by Mike Zeilik at the University of New Mexico, the survey (available at www.flaguide.org) divides the statements into subscales: affect (attitude), cognitive competence, value, and difficulty. Affect relates to positive and negative attitudes about astronomy and science. Cognitive competence describes attitudes about the students' intellectual knowledge and skills when applied to astronomy and science. Value involves attitudes about the usefulness, relevance, and worth of astronomy and science in personal and professional life. Difficulty entails attitudes about the difficulty of astronomy and science as subjects.

The results are shown in Exhibit 9.6, with a 5 indicating strong agreement and a 1 indicating strong disagreement. The responses to Statements 10 and 16 identify the extent to which students like astronomy. Both questions illustrate a difference in the number of students who came into the course anticipating that they would enjoy it and the number who really did. Statements 9, 15, and 20 all address various aspects of students' beliefs in their ability to understand astronomy. The responses show a decrease over time: Students were more confident of their ability to really understand astronomy concepts coming into the course than when they left it. Looking at the overall average, students' attitudes toward astronomy decreased as a result of my course, though as discussed at the beginning of this inquiry, this was not unexpected and in fact matches similar national trends seen in other introductory science courses (e.g., mathematics and computer science). I had hoped that the EDU system would reverse this trend. By taking advantage of opportunities to practice with the course material, students would build mastery over astronomy concepts. This mastery would lead to student confidence in their astronomy knowledge and ultimately a more enjoyable educational experience. Evidently there is more progress to be made in this area.

Exhibit 9.6
Pre- and Post-Test Survey Results for Students' Attitude Toward Astronomy

Statement	Pre-Test	Post-Test	Difference
1. Astronomy is a subject learned quickly by most people.	2.71	2.61	-0.10
2. I (will have, had) trouble understanding astronomy because of how I think.	2.40	2.43	0.03

Statement	Pre-Test	Post-Test	Difference
3. Astronomy concepts (are, were) easy to understand.	3.01	2.74	-0.27
4. Astronomy is irrelevant to my life.	2.49	2.59	0.10
5. I (will get, got) frustrated going over astronomy tests in class.	2.48	2.45	-0.03
6. I (will be, was) under stress during astronomy class.	2.74	2.69	-0.05
7. I (will, do) understand how to apply analytical reasoning to astronomy.	3.27	3.21	-0.06
8. Learning astronomy (requires, required) a great deal of discipline.	3.20	3.11	-0.09
9. I (will have, had) no idea of what's going on in astronomy.	2.24	2.58	0.34
10. I (will, do) like astronomy.	3.63	3.36	-0.27
11. What I learn in astronomy will not be useful in my career.	3.17	3.43	0.26
12. Most people have to learn a new way of thinking to do astronomy.	2.87	2.85	-0.02
13. Astronomy (is, was) highly technical.	3.23	3.10	-0.13
14. I (will feel, felt) insecure when I have to do astronomy homework.	2.42	2.55	0.13
15. I (will find, found) it difficult to understand astronomy concepts.	2.62	2.95	0.33
16. I (will enjoy, enjoyed) taking this astronomy course.	3.58	3.27	-0.31
17. I (will make, made) a lot of errors applying concepts in astronomy.	2.89	2.99	0.10
18. Astronomy (involves, involved) memorizing a massive collection of facts.	3.26	3.35	0.09
19. Astronomy (is, was) a complicated subject.	3.34	3.35	0.01
20. I can learn astronomy.	4.18	2.82	-1.36
21. Astronomy is worthless.	1.88	2.19	0.31
22. I (am, was) scared of astronomy.	2.24	2.48	0.24
23. Scientific conclusions are rarely presented in everyday life.	2.29	2.42	0.13
24. Scientific concepts are easy to understand.	2.84	2.84	0.00

Statement	Pre-Test	Post-Test	Difference
25. Science is not useful to the typical professional.	2.39	2.59	0.20
26. The thought of taking a science course scares me.	2.42	2.61	0.19
27. I like science.	3.10	3.13	0.03
28. I find it difficult to understand scientific concepts.	2.98	2.99	0.01
29. I can learn science.	3.93	3.81	-0.12
30. Scientific skills will make me more employable.	3.55	3.22	-0.33
31. Science is a complicated subject.	3.63	2.58	-1.05
32. I use science in my everyday life.	3.56	3.11	-0.45
33. Scientific thinking is not applicable to my life outside my job.	2.22	2.61	0.39
34. Science should be a required part of my professional training.	2.74	2.82	0.08
Average Response	2.93	2.88	-0.05

COMMENTARY 9.10

Kevin's data can be interpreted in various ways. For instance, his students' more negative attitude may result from a better understanding of what astronomy involves—as Kevin has pointed out, they have made the transition from associating astronomy with learning the names of constellations to understanding that astronomy is a science. The students' attitudes toward the subject might also be influenced by the fact that they were required to put so much time and effort into his course. Yet as his previous data show, students who put this amount of time into their learning did receive higher grades. These findings are significant because we often equate effective teaching with how well students liked a course. In planning your own inquiry, consider that there are instances where no matter how well you teach and how well your students learn, there is the chance that your students will not like your topic in the end. This is certainly true for Kevin, as it is for many astronomers.

Finally, I had my students complete the astronomy diagnostic test (ADT). This survey is designed to measure astronomy content knowledge for undergraduate nonscience majors taking their first astronomy course. The survey (available at www.flaguide.org) was developed by the multi-institutional Collaboration for Astronomy Education Research. Students completed the ADT during the first week of the term, and then again on the last day of the term. The ADT national sample (of approximately 5,500 students) yields an average value of 32.4% for the pre-course test and 47.3% for the post-course test. My class received a 30.0% for the pre-course test and 40.2% for the post-course test. I have struggled with interpreting the low post-course scores. *Does it reflect a lack of student understanding of the concepts?* Maybe. It is possible that practicing with EDU eventually led to familiarity with my (very large) test bank and not a deep conceptual understanding that could be transferred to other problems.

Another contributing factor is the fact that I did not "grade" the ADT. Unlike the EDU survey and the attitudes assessment, the ADT requires concerted effort on the part of the students because it involves content material. I know that some students did not put their best effort into answering the questions. Four of them simply filled down one column of their ADT bubble sheet without even looking at the questions, and at least 10 of them took less time to complete the ADT than I imagine it takes to read the question. On reflection, I just plain over-surveyed them, and they grew tired of it.

COMMENTARY 9.11

In future course offerings, Kevin might consider how the range of student surveys could be distributed and integrated throughout the regular routine of the course. For instance, he might integrate questions from the ADT into the final course examination, or he could replace one of the EDU homework or quiz exercises with the ADT. In this way, students would be motivated to do the assessment because it would affect their final course grade. Kevin might also consider ways that he can share with students his purposes for using such assessments in the course. Students might be more motivated to complete the assessments if he discusses the results and cycles them back into the course.

FINAL REFLECTION

The results of my classroom inquiry clearly support the use of EDU—so much so that as I plan future course offerings, I envision transitioning my course from an instructor-centered format to a student-centered format. To achieve this, I will implement the following changes:

- All lectures will be redone as narrated PowerPoint presentations, with links to animations and other resources that will appear in pop-up windows. These lectures will be placed on the Internet and my students will be responsible for viewing them before class.
- Class time will predominantly be used to emphasize a deeper understanding of the astronomy concepts. For instance, I will show more simulations and animations, share scenes from movies, and/or invite guest speakers to talk to the class.
- Before each class, students will be required to complete a reading quiz over the PowerPoint presentation. Up to now, the reading quizzes consisted of multiple-choice questions. I plan to move to longer, more structured reading quizzes that will add fill-in-the-blank types of questions. Students will still be able to retake the reading quizzes.
- All examinations will be given in the classroom. While I think the EDU system works wonderfully for the reading quizzes and homework, it is somewhat limited for testing aspects of my students' learning. For example, I would love to include questions where I ask students to explain a concept with a well-labeled diagram—this is easy for a student to write on paper, but would be especially difficult to accomplish on the computer.

COMMENTARY 9.12

Kevin's classroom inquiry resulted in several specific ways to improve his course. At a more fundamental level, writing this inquiry portfolio turned out to be a transformational experience for him. Since the time of his inquiry, he has not only implemented all of these changes but gone beyond these suggestions to overhaul major elements of the course. He continues to collect data on how the changes he makes to the course influence student learning. In addition, he has promoted the use of EDU in other departments across campus. Kevin's teaching has received accolades from both peers and students, and as the postscript describes, his course has become a model for how to incorporate student-centered pedagogy into a large survey course.

POSTSCRIPT

Kevin continues to focus on using instructional technology to improve student learning. Many of the innovations he has introduced are made possible by improvements in that technology. He has delivered all of his lectures in PowerPoint with accompanying notes for several years, but he is now importing all of the PowerPoint lectures into Macromedia Breeze, which is more convenient and flexible—for instance, allowing for easier incorporation of Flash animations. Each pre-class lecture still has a corresponding quiz in EDU due before class, but the quiz is now a narrative that summarizes the lecture and asks students to fill in blanks with pull-down menus. These quizzes resemble web pages (with images, tables, and randomized blanks) more than the previous format of a sequence of multiple-choice questions. Kevin's organization of the quiz thus reinforces the structural organization of the lecture material and encourages students to be adequately prepared for class.

Kevin's use of class time has also evolved considerably, with the goal of reinforcing outside learning rather then merely presenting information. He now devotes class time to activities through which students deepen their understanding by using the information conveyed through the pre-class lectures. Although these activities take many forms, Kevin employs three key mechanisms:

- *Peer instruction,* which involves posing conceptual questions to students and having them go through a process of voting and peer discussion as they develop a response. Students benefit from these discussions, and both the students and instructor receive valuable feedback regarding student understanding. Kevin has received substantial funding (from the National Science Foundation) to develop computerized databases of permutable peer instruction questions accompanied by resources to provide explanations to the questions.

- *Groups of students working on exercises collaboratively.* These include database analysis worksheets, discussion questions, and structured tutorials.
- *Use of computer simulations* (developed with funding from the National Science Foundation). These allow students to create mental models of complex physical phenomena that are far beyond their everyday experiences. Every effort is made to use the simulations in an interactive manner by asking students to make predictions regarding what will happen when a variable is changed.

As a result of these changes, Kevin's class time is devoted to developing a deep understanding of the material, and web-based assessment is relegated to a lesser role of practicing with vocabulary and reviewing course concepts.

CHAPTER TEN

CLASSROOM INQUIRY AND SCHOLARLY TEACHING

My inquiry has impacted my students' learning and given me the opportunity to measure and document the course changes. While these activities are completely outside of my disciplinary expertise, I have enjoyed the challenges and the new learning my inquiry has provided.

—Elizabeth Ingraham

Inquiry overview: Elizabeth explores whether visual methods of brainstorming are more effective than verbal methods in her first-year art course.

Highlights: Elizabeth's inquiry brings together many of the elements required for scholarly teaching. She develops a range of linked questions that explore her instructional choices, collects multiple forms of quantitative and qualitative evidence to answer her questions, and uses tables, bar charts, and photographs of student work to present her results. Her inquiry also explores an issue that faculty in certain disciplines often face—the difficulty of evaluating creative student work, especially when many perceive such evaluation as subjective or individualistic.

Course activities used to measure inquiry question: Homework/assignment; project; survey of student opinions; student course evaluation.

Inquiry presentation includes: Self-reflection; bar chart; data table; photograph; example of student work; inclusion of project description.

ABOUT THE COURSE

In my course, Speculative Drawing and Design, students use drawing to investigate, describe, document, and communicate. Students also use drawing to think visually, to develop ideas, and to ask "what if" questions. Students gain skills in construction and hone their craft as they employ basic elements of design (such as positive and negative space, scale, and gesture) in two- and three-dimensional compositions. My aim for the course is for students to become flexible, independent, and self-directed designers. I want them to experience design as a continual process of creating, making, evaluating, and making again and to be able to apply this process to other contexts and to other media in their continuing design education. Exhibit 10.1 shares details of my course.

Exhibit 10.1
Details of Elizabeth's Course

Discipline	Art and Design (Visual Literacy Program)
Course	Speculative Drawing and Design
Course Level	First-year
Number of Students	21 (two sections of the course)
Type of Course	Targeted for majors in studio art, architecture, interior design, graphic design, and textiles
Meeting Time	Three 3-hour studio sessions per week

COMMENTARY 10.1

Elizabeth's goal in her studio art course is to help students learn how to conceptualize and develop their creative ideas. For this reason, Elizabeth's inquiry involves studying the processes by which students learn rather than documenting the students' learning itself.

DEVELOPMENT OF THE INQUIRY

Throughout my course, students must use problem-solving skills or brainstorming. I define *brainstorming* as the ability to generate, communicate, and develop ideas while employing those work habits and personal skills which encourage a creative mind-set. By defining brainstorming as an iterative process of idea generation and development, and not just as a brief activity in the initial stages of a project, I use brainstorming as a shorthand description for creative thinking.

During the course, students complete a series of projects in which they create three-dimensional objects that 1) perform a stated function,

2) have other specifications (such as size or collapsibility), and 3) are made with easily available materials. These projects are otherwise open-ended in terms of what they create. The projects require that students come up with an "idea" for an object (invent and design) and make something which has not existed before (test, revise, fabricate, engineer), while solving functional, structural, and aesthetic problems. The explicit brainstorming tasks that students must complete include:

- Recognizing "what is an idea" and using multiple strategies for generating ideas
- Describing and discussing ideas
- Welcoming all ideas ("good" and "bad") during the idea generation
- Learning how to choose an idea to develop and when and how to modify/abandon an idea
- Persisting until an idea is fully developed

COMMENTARY 10.2

Elizabeth's inquiry will explore the issue of brainstorming for her course, and so her definition provides a needed foundation for readers. Because brainstorming might mean different things to different people, Elizabeth has listed the specific tasks that are involved. Beyond explaining her practices to those outside of her discipline, Elizabeth's breakdown of general goals into specific elements will help her to develop measures to determine whether students have learned these tasks.

PUTTING THE ISSUE INTO CONTEXT

The goal of my classroom inquiry is to investigate the first studio project that students complete in my course: the Cooperative Connector Project. In this project, students work in pairs and use inexpensive and found materials to make a wearable connector which joins body parts. Exhibit 10.2 gives the project description that I provide to my students. The Cooperative Connector Project requires students to solve a difficult problem within a short time frame, while working in cooperation with others with differing perspectives and dealing with external conditions that are not completely within their control.

Exhibit 10.2
Details of Elizabeth's Cooperative Connector Project

1. Using any inexpensive or found materials (Tyvek, fabric, vinyl, paper, corrugated cardboard, metal, wood, plastic, etc.), make a cooperative connector that joins you and your partner at two locations on your bodies and that functions to keep you and your partner joined.

2. This is a collaborative project. You will draw names in studio to determine your partner(s) and the body locations to be connected.

3. Your connector has the following required elements:
   - Each person will draw a location and mirror that location on his or her partner's body. Thus, two people will be connecting at two locations. (You will have left-right symmetry.)
   - Your connector must be designed and fabricated (articulated, manipulated) by you, not ready-made, although it may incorporate ready-made components. (It should also not be simply a recreation of an existing device in other materials or at a larger scale.)
   - You must use a rigid material and a flexible material and a textured material.
   - Your connector must intentionally connect to your partner and must be supported without your holding it.
   - You and your partner must be able to move while wearing your connector without it falling off or breaking.
   - Your connector may not touch the ground between you and your partner.
   - Each connection must be reasonably direct and between 12" and 24" (approximately) in length.

COMMENTARY 10.3

The inclusion of the project description helps readers to understand what is required of students to complete the project. It also makes explicit the criteria by which the students' projects will be judged.

The Cooperative Connector Project is the most difficult course project for students and for me as the teacher. To meet the minimum requirements, students need to "get an idea," communicate this idea to me and to the class, and work cooperatively and collaboratively, which intensifies the need for clear communication. Exhibit 10.3 gives the grading criteria I use and share ahead of time with my students. To come up with a good idea (i.e., a highly successful solution) students often must push their thinking past the literal to the metaphorical. It is relatively easy for students to make a picture or a representation of something which already exists, but it can be very difficult for them to invent something new or to work in a more stylized or abstract way. My challenge with the Cooperative Connector Project is getting students to make something visual to see and to talk about as soon as possible so that they can get useful feedback. Thus, I ask students to use drawings or models to talk about their ideas.

EXHIBIT 10.3
Grading Criteria for the Connector Project

- Your connector meets the *basic project requirements*.
- You used *excellent craft*. (Your connector is sturdy, wearable, and functional; joints are strong; cuts are clean; there is no visible glue or tape unless the tape is used as a design element.)
- Your connection is *intentional* and the *transitions* between your connector and your body are well thought out and well designed.
- You have a strong *overall design* or composition. (Your design is *volumetric*, carefully considers *both positive and negative space* and the distance or proximity between you and your partner, and has a *clear [exaggerated] gesture*.)
- You *pushed* beyond the expected response in craft or design or function. (Your engineering is especially inventive or your materials are especially effective or your craft is especially exquisite.)

COMMENTARY 10.4

Note that Elizabeth shares the grading criteria with her students ahead of time to help them focus their efforts—the students know what will be expected of them as they work on their project. Her inclusion of the grading criteria as part of her inquiry complements the project description so that readers also know what is expected from the project and how it will be evaluated. The grading criteria also emphasize key components of the process in which she hopes students will engage—namely brainstorming ideas and receiving feedback on this brainstorming for an improved final product.

During past terms, I have observed that students are often reluctant to use visual communication. For instance, during my desk critiques of their work, a student will begin with a long verbal description of his or her problem. When I interrupt and ask, "Where's your drawing?" the student will respond, "My drawing? Oh, my drawing . . ." The student then searches through piles of papers and pulls out a beautiful drawing. This drawing is often gestural and expressive and suggests possibilities which words do not. The drawing shows me where the student is trying to go so that we can discuss how to get there.

I believe that the more I insist that students present their ideas visually and "talk about" their design problems with diagrams or models, the more fully developed their solutions will be. Useful feedback requires that we "see" the same thing, and words alone are inadequate for describing visual conditions. Speakers and hearers can have vastly different assumptions based on the same verbal description (whether written or spoken). Visual aids, whether drawings, models, material samples, or the work in progress, remove much of the ambiguity of verbal communication so that communication is more efficient and feedback immediately becomes more focused.

My theory is that visual methods of brainstorming are more effective than verbal. They are certainly more effective from my viewpoint, since they make my job easier. *But are they more effective from a student's point of view? Is there any relationship between the quality of students' brainstorming and the quality of their finished projects? Are students using visual methods to brainstorm, even if I'm not always seeing evidence of this? Are they reluctant to draw or use visual imagery or just reluctant to show these visuals to anyone else?*

COMMENTARY 10.5

Elizabeth's inquiry focuses on the value of the brainstorming process both from her perspective and from that of her students. While Elizabeth intuitively feels that she is able to respond more productively to visual brainstorming, she wants to confirm her intuition as a teacher and to determine the extent to which students find this approach productive as well.

INQUIRY HYPOTHESIS

Using my Cooperative Connector Project, I want to ask the central question: *Are visual methods of brainstorming more effective than verbal methods?* To answer this question, I need to address a series of subquestions:

- What methods do students use to brainstorm? Are these methods visual, verbal, or both?
- Do students prefer visual or verbal methods of brainstorming?
- Do students find visual or verbal methods more effective?
- Is there any discrepancy between the methods students prefer and the methods students find most effective? Or between the methods students use and the methods they prefer or find most effective? What reasons do students give for choosing the methods they prefer? The methods they find most effective?
- What types of visual evidence can students provide of their most effective brainstorming methods?
- Is there any relationship between the quality of a student's brainstorming evidence and the strength of the completed project?

COMMENTARY 10.6

On first reading, it might seem that Elizabeth is asking too many questions. However, if you look further at how she has crafted her list, the answer to each question builds directly on the previous one. In a way, Elizabeth's questions are modeling the type of brainstorming that she hopes her students will engage in. By generating a full range of questions, Elizabeth is trying to approach her inquiry from as many different angles and perspectives as possible. In the end, she will collect enough data to answer her central question.

INVESTIGATIVE PLAN

I used three primary sources of data to explore my inquiry question. First, after the Cooperative Connector Project was completed, I had students complete a survey (Exhibit 10.4) identifying the brainstorming methods they used from a checklist of 10 methods, 5 of which were visual and 5 of which were verbal. (The characterization of the methods as visual or verbal was not provided on the survey.) Students then specified their 3 most *preferred* methods, the 3 most *effective* methods, and stated their reasons for their choices. Although students worked in groups for the project, each of the 21 students submitted a separate survey.

EXHIBIT 10.4

Student Survey of Brainstorming Approaches

Please check which brainstorming methods you used:

☐ Making lists

☐ Looking at images from books, magazines, or the Internet

☐ Emailing my partner

☐ Talking on the phone myself/ with my partner

☐ Drawing

☐ Exploring found objects/materials

☐ Discussing with my partner using visual aids

☐ Discussing with my partner without visual aids

☐ Drawing on photos of partner

☐ Writing

Of the methods that you used, which do you prefer? (Rank your top three.)

1.

2.

3.

Why?

Which do you find the most effective? (Rank your top three.)

1.

2.

3.

Why?

COMMENTARY 10.7

This survey is both easy and effective. It does not take too much time for students to complete and it uses a combination of simple checkboxes, rankings, and comments. The only change we might suggest would be to add an "other" box for students to specify an approach that Elizabeth did not include. Beyond providing useful feedback to Elizabeth, this survey also helps students to reflect more fully on the processes that they used to complete their project. In other words, simply taking the survey has the pedagogical potential of helping students to think more consciously about their learning.

Students also submitted one page of *visual evidence* of their most effective brainstorming methods. There were no requirements concerning the form of this evidence, beyond stating that it had to be effective for the student. Neither the survey nor the visual evidence was graded. Finally, the project partners were photographed demonstrating their completed connectors project, and I assigned a project grade.

INTERPRETING AND EVALUATING FINDINGS

Exhibit 10.5 shows the percentage of students who *used, preferred,* and thought *effective* the 10 brainstorming approaches solicited in the survey. The brainstorming approaches, whether visual or verbal, and the corresponding data series label (used in Exhibit 10.5) are given in Exhibit 10.6. Overall, every student used a combination of visual and verbal methods to brainstorm and no students used only verbal or only visual methods. No student used less than four methods, and the average number of methods used was six. The three most used methods were all visual (drawing, discussing with visuals, and exploring materials).

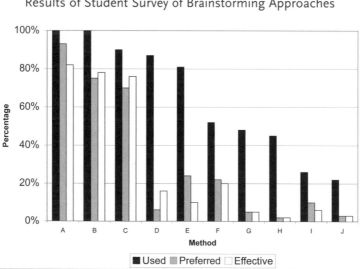

EXHIBIT 10.5
Results of Student Survey of Brainstorming Approaches

Exhibit 10.6
Brainstorming Approaches

Method	Visual or Verbal	Data Series in Exhibit 10.5
Drawing	Visual	A
Discussing (with partner) with visuals	Visual	B
Exploring materials	Visual	C
Discussing (with partner) without visuals	Verbal	D
Making lists	Verbal	E
Looking at images	Visual	F
Talking on the phone with partner	Verbal	G
Writing	Verbal	H
Drawing on photos of student and partner	Visual	I
Emailing partner	Verbal	J

Students clearly preferred visual methods of brainstorming. The three most *preferred* methods were visual (drawing, discussing with visuals, and exploring materials). The three least preferred methods were verbal (discussing without visuals, talking on the phone, and emailing). Students found the visual methods of brainstorming more effective. The three most effective methods were all visual (drawing, discussing with visuals, and exploring materials).

There is no significant discrepancy between the methods students *preferred* and the methods students found most *effective*. Interestingly, I had expected that students might strongly prefer using certain methods even if they discovered that other methods were more effective.

There is a significant discrepancy between the methods students *used* and the methods they identified as *preferred* or *effective*. Of the 10 methods used, 5 methods (4 verbal and 1 visual) were neither preferred nor found effective by any significant number of students. I suspect that students tried, but discarded, a number of methods. This is not surprising as I suggested they use a wide variety of brainstorming methods. Looking at the 5 methods that were the most used, 3 methods (drawing, discussing with visuals, exploring materials), all visual, were the most used, the most preferred, and the most effective of all brainstorming methods.

COMMENTARY 10.8

Elizabeth's presentation of the survey results in a single graph provides a simple and clear view of what students used, preferred, and found effective. This graph gives Elizabeth clear and useful evidence for understanding the students' brainstorming choices, which she can draw on when she revises the course in future offerings. If Elizabeth were interested in publishing her results, she possibly would need to perform a statistical inference test (e.g., difference of proportions) to see if the observed differences are statistically significant.

Students' written comments on the reasons for choosing each method were brief and their reasons for preference and for effectiveness were often identical. Reasons were all expressed in positive terms, and many students simply stated that a particular method "works for me" or "inspires me" or "I like (method)." Exhibit 10.7 groups the responses into general categories. Three visual methods (drawing, discussing with visuals, and exploring materials) generated the most comments. Not surprisingly, these three methods were also students' most *preferred* and most *effective* methods.

EXHIBIT 10.7
Reason Students Gave for Preferring a Method or Thinking It Effective

Reason	Percentage of Students (Preferred)	Percentage of Students (Effective)	Visual or Verbal
Visuals make ideas easier to understand/communicate.	61%	45%	Visual
Drawing works for me/I like to draw.	58%	65%	Visual
Materials inspire me/I need to work with materials.	55%	71%	Visual
Discussing with visuals works for me.	35%	52%	Visual

Reason	Percentage of Students (Preferred)	Percentage of Students (Effective)	Visual or Verbal
Looking at images inspires me.	16%	19%	Visual
Making lists works for me/I like to make lists.	16%	10%	Verbal
Drawing on photos helps me understand the site.	6%	0%	Visual
Discussing without visuals works for me.	0%	10%	Verbal

COMMENTARY 10.9

Rather than present the cumulative list of student comments, Elizabeth chose to classify them into one of eight categories and then to present the class percentage for each category. You might find a similar classification strategy to be effective in interpreting and representing the results of your own inquiry project. Elizabeth could also share these statistics with her students as the basis for a follow-up discussion about their choices and as a way to further engage students in reflecting on their artistic processes.

I also asked students to provide one page of visual evidence of their most effective brainstorming method(s). Partners had to choose their own evidence of what was most effective for him or her, but visual evidence was not otherwise defined. Ninety percent of the students submitted a drawing. Of these, 68% accompanied it with text—ranging from one word or a label to brief questions or measurements to longer lists, most often of associations or of possible materials. Exhibit 10.8 shares examples of the range of the students' brainstorming drawings. Drawings ranged from the stylized and gestural to more detailed technical drawings exploring construction methods and details, and the photo of the partners also included drawing. On reflection, the fact that I received a high percentage of drawings is consistent with students' preference for visual methods and, I hope, reflects the course expectation that students use visual methods to design and to communicate effectively.

EXHIBIT 10.8

Samples of Brainstorming Evidence Drawings

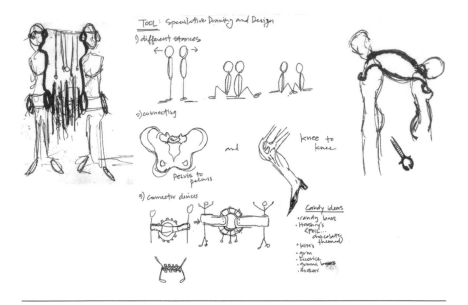

COMMENTARY 10.10

The inclusion of examples of her students' brainstorming evidence showcases exactly what students turned in. Elizabeth is demonstrating what she herself pointed out earlier in her inquiry: A picture is worth a thousand words.

To see if there is any relationship between the quality of a student's brainstorming evidence and the strength of his or her completed project, I needed to assess a project's quality. I defined *quality* as visual richness and complexity and ranked the samples as low, average, or high. Once I started looking at their work, I found this definition to be too ambiguous and subjective—if it included communicating clearly then it overlapped with usefulness; if it included expressiveness or visual presence, then I was too influenced by the seductiveness of a drawing. Recognizing the limited usefulness of this definition, I nevertheless proceeded with my analysis of the student projects to see what insight they could provide.

COMMENTARY 10.11

Here Elizabeth notes a common issue that teachers face. In the process of assessing students' projects, she found that her criteria were not specific enough to enable her to make meaningful distinctions among them. Due to the limits of time and necessity, Elizabeth still used the criteria for assessing the projects, but she now knows that in future offerings of her course, revising the criteria sheets will make her assessment easier.

I expected that there would be a clear correspondence between the quality of a student's brainstorming evidence and the strength of his or her completed project. Instead, there was no such relationship, whether considering the group as a whole or looking at individual samples. (This finding suggests the need for further study.)

I used the project description and my grading rubric to gauge the strength of the completed project. All the projects received 40 points or above (out of 50 points possible) and the overall quality of the completed projects was high. However, the brainstorming evidence varied much more in quality than the projects themselves. Looking at the brainstorming evidence samples, 19% were low quality, 55% were average quality, and 26% were high quality. In comparison, the projects were all above average. Thus, the projects were richer overall than the brainstorming evidence would suggest. Since I chose not to impose any guidelines on this brainstorming evidence, there were no specifications as to format or craft. This evidence was just a snapshot of their learning process, chosen by the students, and not edited or composed. Students knew that they were not being graded on this submission.

Overall, I found that while some strong projects also had higher quality (richer) brainstorming evidence, some did not, and conversely, some weaker projects nevertheless had rich brainstorming evidence. Exhibit 10.9 shows one team that had rich brainstorming evidence and a very strong project. They converged on an idea (constructed vertebrae) very quickly but also considered, tested, and discarded multiple methods of construction and attachment (transition) to the body.

EXHIBIT 10.9
Strong Student Project With Rich Brainstorming Evidence

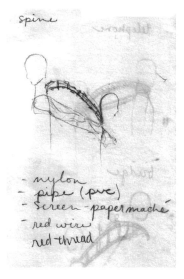

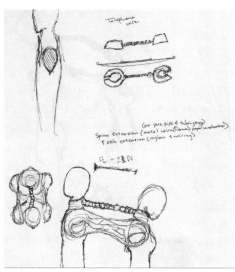

Exhibit 10.10 shows a student team that had strong brainstorming evidence but the weakest project overall, because they did not push beyond the aggregation of a pre-formed found object (Chinese lanterns), the use of a conventional crafted form (origami cranes), and an easy method of transitioning or connecting to the body (free-form draping). Thus, what is undeveloped in this brainstorming evidence is also what is undeveloped in the project—the transition to the body of each partner and the manipulation or transformation of the pleated volumetric forms of the lanterns.

EXHIBIT 10.10
Weak Student Project With Strong Brainstorming Evidence

Overall, while I did not find the relationship I expected between the brainstorming evidence and the completed projects, the brainstorming evidence gave me a deeper insight into the project and the students' processes.

COMMENTARY 10.12

Not only does Elizabeth explain the final grades that the projects received, but her reflective discussion and the inclusion of two examples provide a window into her students' work, her grading of it, and her overall classroom inquiry.

FINAL REFLECTION

The goal of my classroom inquiry was to answer the following central question: *Are visual methods of brainstorming more effective than verbal methods?* The short answer is yes, visual methods are more effective than verbal methods. An overwhelming majority of my students (68%) found visual methods more effective. The three most effective methods were all visual. These same visual methods were also the methods that students most preferred and most used. Conversely, the three least effective methods were all verbal.

In terms of the subquestions that I posed:

- *What methods do students use to brainstorm? Are these methods visual, verbal, or both?* All students used a combination of visual and verbal brainstorming methods, although visual methods were used more frequently than verbal methods. The three most used brainstorming methods were all visual.
- *Do students prefer visual or verbal methods of brainstorming?* Students preferred visual methods of brainstorming. The three most preferred methods were all visual ones and the three least preferred methods were all verbal ones.
- *Do students find visual or verbal methods of brainstorming more effective?* Students found visual methods of brainstorming more effective. The three most effective methods were all visual ones and the three least effective methods were all verbal ones.
- *Is there any discrepancy between the methods students prefer and the methods students find most effective? Or between the methods students use and the methods they prefer or find most effective?* There was no significant discrepancy between the methods students preferred and the methods they found most effective. There was a significant discrepancy between the methods students used and the methods students then preferred or found effective. Of the 10 methods used, there were 5 methods (only 1 of which was visual) that were neither preferred nor found effective. However, 3 methods, all visual, were the most used, the most preferred, and the most effective.
- *What reasons do students give for the methods they prefer? The methods they find most effective?* Reasons were grouped into eight general categories and were all expressed in positive terms.
- *Can students present useful brainstorming evidence of their most effective brainstorming methods? What types of evidence can students provide?* All students submitted visual evidence of their brainstorming methods.
- *Is there any relationship between the quality of a student's brainstorming evidence and the strength of the completed project?* There was no consistent relationship between the quality of a student's brainstorming evidence and the strength of the completed project. The brainstorming evidence varied more widely in quality than the projects themselves. While the projects were all above average, the evidence samples varied from low to high quality. However, comparing the brainstorming evidence to the completed projects provided insight into the students' process and their project development.

One unexpected benefit of my classroom inquiry is that I now have a rich resource of visual evidence of students' brainstorming methods. I plan to use this visual evidence in future offerings of my course, showing the brainstorming examples in conjunction with the completed projects. I hope that this will help students better understand the project development from initial idea to completed connector and will make the process of visual communication less intimidating to students by showing how simple drawings and models can clarify complex ideas.

I began my classroom inquiry with the belief that visual methods of brainstorming were more effective. My belief was pragmatic—the sooner the students and I see a drawing, a photograph, or a material sample, the sooner we can give useful feedback. I knew that I valued visual communication. What I didn't realize until this inquiry was that students also recognize the value of, and prefer, visual communication. Looking forward, if visual methods of brainstorming are more effective, and my investigation shows that they are, what can I do to further encourage these methods? *That is, what can I do to encourage drawing and other methods of visual exploration and visual communication?*

COMMENTARY 10.13

Elizabeth's inquiry answered her question and raised new questions to pursue in future offerings of the course. Now that she has confirmed her intuition that visual methods are most effective and preferred by her students, she can begin developing a data bank of visual brainstorming examples that she can share with her students. In future offerings of her course, she might explore more fully the relationship between effective brainstorming and the quality of the final projects. That is, if students' visual brainstorming is not as rich as it might be, she could consider ways to more fully incorporate this component into her class, such as counting the brainstorming as part of the grade. Or, if students' brainstorming does not lead to a strong final project, she might engage students in discussions about why this is the case. Finally, it's important to note that Elizabeth's inquiry has the potential to shape her teaching of other courses as she expands using visual techniques for developing creativity. Elizabeth is well into her journey as a scholarly teacher.

CHAPTER ELEVEN

BEGINNING YOUR
SCHOLARLY JOURNEY

EFFECTIVE TEACHING ENTAILS more than simply delivering a lecture with coherence and clarity or sustaining students' attention with class activities. An effective teacher has a positive impact on students inside the classroom, promotes student enthusiasm and inquiry outside the classroom, and participates in efforts to improve the direction, visibility, and importance of teaching at one's school. The inquiry examples in the previous chapters demonstrate how teachers have used their classroom inquiry projects to evaluate, improve, and document their teaching and its impact on their students' learning. As illustrated by the range of examples, how one carries out such inquiry differs from teacher to teacher. No two classroom inquiry projects are the same. Each inquiry is specific to the teacher, the course being taught, the students taking the course, and the inquiry question being explored.

By showcasing actual inquiry examples, we hope that we have eliminated some of the mystery from the process and motivated you to carry out your own classroom inquiry. To get you started on a similar scholarly journey, this chapter highlights some lessons learned from the inquiry examples, provides some practical advice for framing your inquiry, describes the different venues through which you might disseminate your work, and points to additional resources related to postsecondary conversations about classroom inquiry and the scholarship of teaching.

LESSONS CONCERNING CLASSROOM INQUIRY

The showcased inquiry examples come from a broad range of disciplines and levels, from art to construction management, from general education courses for first-year students to professional training for graduate students. Nevertheless, the teachers of these courses have faced many of the same issues: how best to deal with students' misconceptions about a discipline (D'Andra and Kevin, Chapters 6 and 9), how to ensure that students understand and have internalized the information rather than simply repeating what they think the teacher wants to hear (Frauke and Carolyn, Chapters 3 and 4), or how to push students to apply what they have learned in class through carrying out a project whether individually (Frauke, Chapter 3) or as part of a team (Tim, Chapter 7). In this respect, disciplinary topics and course level are not so important as the common questions we face as teachers. And just as we learn from the inquiry of others, our own inquiry can benefit other teachers when it is written, documented, and made public to an audience of readers.

In addition to highlighting some of the teaching issues we all face, these examples also demonstrate some important principles concerning classroom inquiry. First, many of them demonstrate the benefits of using both quantitative and qualitative measures to assess student learning, or of combining the objective criteria you use as a teacher to evaluate student learning with the students' subjective perception of their own learning. As we said in the first chapter, a well-designed inquiry includes a variety of assessment techniques to give a balanced and well-rounded understanding of what is going on in the classroom.

Second, the methods of inquiry we have described can be applied to a range of questions. *Are you interested in examining the whole course or a specific unit or topic taught within the course? In assessing pedagogical approaches or assessment techniques? In determining the content and amount of student learning, the process by which students learn, or the impact of your teaching on the acquisition of skills or of attitudes, values, and understanding?* These methods can be used to address any of these emphases.

Third, as is clear from all the inquiry examples, effective inquiry almost always leads to new insights into how to improve the course the next time you teach it. This does not mean that there is something "wrong" with your present approach to teaching; instead, this statement simply reflects the fact that excellent teaching involves growth and development. Classroom inquiry is a tool that outstanding teachers can use to target more efficiently those areas where they can best improve the quantity and quality of their students' learning.

Finally, classroom inquiry is a continuing journey. It doesn't stop at the end of the term but can be pursued for as long as you wish to investigate an issue. Sometimes, as in Tim's case (Chapter 7), the inquiry does not answer your initial question fully; more often, as in many of the highlighted cases, the initial hypothesis is either supported or rejected, but the inquiry itself raises new questions and issues that might be the subject of further inquiry. In this sense, scholarly teaching can become a continuing journey, in which the pleasure and reward comes from the travel itself rather than from reaching the final destination.

PRACTICAL ADVICE FOR CONDUCTING YOUR INQUIRY

Since the lessons drawn from the inquiry examples of the previous chapters may still seem rather abstract and general, we have several practical suggestions for conducting your classroom inquiry.

Work with faculty peers to improve your success.

We have found that teachers are often more successful with classroom inquiry when they have a partner or a community of colleagues with whom to share and receive feedback on their projects. To improve the quality of your inquiry and to increase your enjoyment of it, we strongly suggest that you link with others performing similar classroom inquiries. If you are interested in examining your classroom from a disciplinary perspective, you can partner with a department colleague or with a colleague from another institution who teaches a similar course or who faces a similar issue in his or her teaching. But it is not necessary that your peer teach the same course or even be in your same discipline. In fact, we have found that our own inquiry projects have been immeasurably enriched by the feedback of colleagues outside our departments. Thus, you may find a peer partner through a college teaching circle, or participate in a focus group sponsored by your school's teaching and learning center.

Having colleagues offer insight into and peer critique of your classroom inquiry can add to your motivation for carrying out the project work. Teachers often find that building "teaching connections" with peers through discussions of teaching questions, teaching methods, and approaches and strategies for assessing student learning is the most enjoyable aspect of a classroom inquiry effort. Exhibit 11.1 lists some of the goals you might have as you meet with peers to focus your efforts and to learn about their goals.

EXHIBIT 11.1

Key Meetings and Objectives When Working With Peer Partner(s)

Meeting Theme	What to Share	Meeting Objectives
Problem definition	Share *Inquiry Steps 1, 2, and 3*	Your peers can offer suggestions for focusing your inquiry effort and/or can offer insight on improving your hypothesis.
Investigation plan	Share *Inquiry Steps 4, 5, and 6*	In addition to being able to divide up and report on the relevant literature, your peers will be able to comment on your proposed data collection strategy and possibly walk you through your effort in seeking institutional review board approval.
Teaching the course	During *Inquiry Step 7*	While teaching the course, your peers can offer ideas if you find that your inquiry project goals are not working. They also can encourage you to be diligent in collecting your course data.
Analysis and conclusions	Share *Inquiry Steps 8 and 9*	Your peers can offer a critical review of your inquiry project and offer suggestions that strengthen your presentation.

Be realistic about the time needed for your classroom inquiry.
We often tell students that they need time and commitment to succeed in our courses. The same is true for your success in completing a classroom inquiry project. This notion often runs counter to a common assumption, usually held by university administrators, that meaningful assessment of learning can be completed and written up as a report in a single afternoon. In order to do a thorough inquiry, you must formulate a significant inquiry question, define a proper investigative strategy, collect the needed data during the course, and then analyze the data and develop your conclusions. This process requires time, often a teacher's most precious commodity. Frequently teachers ask: *How much time should I set*

aside? This question is not easy to answer since your previous experience in performing classroom inquiry is often a defining factor. For instance, a teacher experienced in reflecting on his or her own teaching might jump immediately from *Inquiry Step 1* (reflecting on course background, history, and development) to *Inquiry Step 3* (defining an inquiry hypothesis), while less experienced individuals will need to spend more time on *Inquiry Step 2* (identifying an issue to investigate). *Inquiry Step 5* (relating your inquiry to what has been done before) may require a lot of effort, but you may decide to skip this step completely. Correspondingly, submitting a plan to your school's institutional review board, *Inquiry Step 6* (seeking institutional approval and student consent), may delay your effort.

At a more fundamental level, serious reflection—and the writing through which that reflection is articulated—will always require an investment of time. But we are firm believers in the saying, "You get what you pay for." The teachers we have worked with all say that the benefits—improved student learning, more efficient use of planning and assessment time, and more effective course and curriculum design—more than outweigh the cost of the time they put into developing their classroom inquiry. And just as importantly, their classroom inquiry has stimulated intellectual engagement to increase their enjoyment of a job they already loved.

How does the inquiry process fit into the rhythms of the college term, whether semester, trimester, or quarter? In general, *Inquiry Steps 1 to 6* should be done before you start teaching the course. In our experience, teachers often change their course design (e.g., modifying assessment strategies, changing classroom practices, incorporating a new instructional approach, developing grading criteria, etc.) as a result of planning their classroom inquiry. Indeed, many teachers say that their courses are often improved simply through preparing for their classroom inquiries. For this reason, we suggest that you start planning your inquiry project at least three months before the beginning of the term. This amount of time allows you the opportunity to truly reflect on and develop your classroom inquiry project and to make any changes before the term begins. *Inquiry Step 7* involves teaching your course and collecting the data. If your inquiry question encompasses the entire course, then you cannot start *Inquiry Steps 8* (interpreting and evaluating your findings) and *9* (reflecting on the inquiry process) until after the course is complete, thus stretching your classroom inquiry beyond the end of the term.

A focused question is often best.

It is often easier—especially during your first few classroom inquiry projects—to define, test, and analyze a very narrow and focused classroom question. For example, rather than exploring the general impact of a semester-long group project, you could divide this inquiry into several smaller issues or questions to explore during successive course offerings. In the first iteration, you could explore how the project reflects students' abilities to apply course concepts. Later, you could analyze how team composition influences the final group project or how to incorporate students' evaluation of their teammates' contributions into the project grade. Many teachers find that what they originally considered a focused question often raises numerous subquestions that can take them onto several different inquiry paths.

Consider both your own and outside interests when choosing an issue to explore.

When formulating your classroom inquiry project, address a question that genuinely interests you—one that you are passionate about answering. But there needs to be a balance. Your passion for a topic or question might seem trivial or obtuse to colleagues. Depending on the ultimate objective of your inquiry—for personal growth or for an external audience—this outside influence can have some impact in determining your inquiry question. For instance, if your academic department will soon be going through an accreditation or program review, then perhaps your inquiry could help serve this review by exploring the quality of student learning in your course rather than looking more narrowly at the value of a specific instructional practice. As we often tell our students, research usually contributes to or builds on an existing conversation. Thinking about which teaching conversations you would like to support will help you to determine how to focus your inquiry.

Share your question.

Even without an answer, your inquiry question is sometimes such a good one that it is worth telling others about. Not only will they be able to offer feedback, but also your discussions will highlight the significance of your teaching and your students' learning. If we want to elevate the importance and respect that colleagues give to teaching, then we ourselves need to start talking about teaching in a "scholarly" way. Sharing teaching inquiry questions can help make our colleagues more knowledgeable about the criteria for improved student performance and can serve as a means for developing a common language for documenting and assessing teaching as intellectual work. As an example, consider sharing with a colleague your grading rubric for one of your classroom assignments. Doing so will introduce him or her to using rubrics and possibly will enable you to have a substantive conversation about what each of you expects from your students and how you each measure it.

Brainstorm, but don't reinvent the wheel.

When defining your investigative plan, the better and more encompassing your strategy is for collecting data, the more easily you will be able to draw meaningful conclusions. But you don't need to come up with your inquiry plan in isolation, and you can find practical suggestions for doing classroom inquiry from many different sources. Talking with other teachers is one of the best ways to find new methods of data collection and analysis that will improve your inquiry. Reviewing other examples of classroom inquiry projects also can be useful, as can browsing through scholarly publications (e.g., journals, books) that focus on classroom assessment techniques.

Make classroom inquiry a priority.

It is important that you start your classroom inquiry project sooner rather than later. A common mistake is to spend so much time thinking and planning that you never get around to actually doing it or finishing it. There's no one else to do the project for you. Since you are the one who cares, the drive to do it must come from within you. Perhaps you are thinking, *But I was told I am supposed to focus on my (disciplinary) research.* This concern is common and valid. But through your classroom inquiry, you are seeking to learn more about your teaching, and the results will have an impact not only on the course that is the focus of your inquiry but also on your teaching more generally. As a consequence, your classroom inquiry project will often have a large payoff in minimizing your need to make changes or major modifications to future offerings of the course—10 hours spent now could save you 30 hours over the next two years. Moreover, once you've engaged in the classroom inquiry process, you are often better prepared in the teaching of all your courses.

You may need to learn new skills.

Depending on your disciplinary area, you may well need to learn some new skills to successfully complete your inquiry project. For example, an art teacher might need to learn how to use a spreadsheet for analyzing student performance data. Or an engineering teacher might have to learn how to design a student survey. Don't be afraid to admit your lack of knowledge and seek out resources that can help you. Working with peer teachers outside your department or program can be especially helpful in this regard.

Assess your instructional abilities.

What you do in the classroom may influence your inquiry project in a way you did not foresee. You need to be aware of this possibility and take steps to reduce the likelihood of unintended consequences. For example, the disappointing results of introducing a new assessment technique may be due more to your inexperience with using it than with the method itself. Indeed, your classroom inquiry might help you to discern why the technique is not working in the way that you had hoped. Rather than giving up on the technique, you might want to obtain additional expertise in applying it effectively, and then reexamine its impact in your classroom.

Be honest about your bias.

I tried that before and it does not work is a common assertion made by some teachers. If you begin your inquiry project with a strong bias regarding the outcome, chances are you will directly or indirectly influence the final results. When defining an inquiry question, you need to choose an issue that you want to answer, but also one for which you are open to a range of results. If you are studying the impact of a semester-long project on student learning, for instance, are you prepared to hear student feedback that two shorter projects might work more effectively in helping them to apply course concepts? Being open to the results of your inquiry might lead you to changing your teaching methods, developing different course assignments, or rethinking overall course objectives.

Be prepared for detours and dead ends in your scholarly journey.

Perhaps the student data that you collected during the term does not measure the learning that you thought it would. Or possibly the service-learning project that you had your students working on needed to be stopped due to an issue outside of your control. Bennett (2001) notes that "classroom inquiry work is not always neat and tidy" (p. 21). Rather then letting these roadblocks discourage you, try to see them as positive developments. Consider other journeys you have gone on—oftentimes the dead ends or detours that we face are the most memorable. When you sense things are out of control—*stop*. Sit quietly, relax, reestablish your priorities in writing, decide what action to take, and then begin again.

FROM SCHOLARLY TEACHING TO THE SCHOLARSHIP OF TEACHING AND LEARNING

The answer to a classroom inquiry question often leads to more questions: *How can I do it better? What would happen if I changed it? What if I removed it?* These new questions enhance your intellectual discovery and stimulate you to continue the journey of scholarly teaching. The inquiries featured in this book were written by scholarly teachers in order to improve their own classroom practice, and the authors did not intend them to meet the more rigorous design expectations associated with the scholarship of teaching and learning. Their inquiries were conducted with varying degrees of depth and detail appropriate in each case to the teacher's specific needs. For this reason, it is best to think of classroom inquiry as enabling investigation at many different levels and appropriate for a variety of audiences.

There is a broad range for classroom inquiry that lies between looking at a specific question for your own improvement as a teacher and publishing your inquiry for a broader audience in a journal focused on teaching. You are the one who determines where in this range your inquiry will fall. For some, the path may lead from scholarly teaching to the scholarship of teaching and learning. As we said in Chapter 1, the scholarship of teaching and learning differs from scholarly teaching in that it makes explicit use of the growing literature of teaching and learning in its inquiry, and it is intended for a broader audience outside one's school and sometimes one's discipline. As the audience for your inquiry broadens, the expectations for the scope and significance of your inquiry will increase. As with the publication of disciplinary-based research, the most rigorous standards for evaluating classroom inquiry apply when you wish to publish it. Outside reviewers of a manuscript describing your inquiry project will require a strong investigative plan, appropriate analysis of the results, a high level and quality of writing, and an inquiry that builds on or complements others' work. Depending on the goals you have for doing your inquiry, there are a variety of ways, from informal to peer reviewed, in which you can disseminate your work.

MODELS FOR DISSEMINATING YOUR INQUIRY WORK

As academics, we often focus on the traditional methods of dissemination such as journal articles or conference presentations. Depending on the reward system in your department and school, these are perhaps the most appropriate means for you to explore. However, there are other ways to make your classroom inquiry work visible. Exhibit 11.2 shares a list of potential methods and audiences for disseminating your inquiry.

EXHIBIT 11.2

Potential Methods and Audiences for Dissemination

Method of Dissemination	Where	Potential Audience
Oral report	Your classroom	Current students
	Department meeting	Department colleagues
	Teaching circle	Teaching colleagues
Poster	Your classroom	Current students
	Display within your department	Current students Future students Department colleagues
	Present at a conference	Disciplinary and teaching peers
Formal presentation	Campus event	Current and future students Campus colleagues School administrators
	Disciplinary conference	Disciplinary peers
	Teaching conference	Teaching peers
Course portfolio	Web site	Disciplinary and teaching peers Current and future students Campus colleagues School administrators
Scholarly publication	Disciplinary journal	Disciplinary peers
	Teaching-related journal	Teaching peers
Manuscript	Through a publisher	National audience

You might describe your classroom inquiry project and its results to students in your course, to members of a teaching circle, or to colleagues at a department meeting. Many of the teachers highlighted in the previous chapters explicitly involved students in their classroom inquiries, making students co-participants in the inquiry process and sharing the results with current and future students. Students often comment positively on such experiences, excited that their teachers care enough about their teaching to conduct such inquiries.

Next, you could develop your results into a poster or handout that you share with students or display publicly. Carolyn (Chapter 4) displays her results on a poster shown at research conferences at her school. A formal presentation at a conference or a campus event allows you an opportunity to communicate to larger audiences regarding your inquiry, its results, and its impact on you and your students. A course portfolio (Bernstein, Burnett, Goodburn, & Savory, 2006) is a reflective investigation of how course structures, teaching techniques, and assessment strategies enhance or detract from student learning. As such, it provides a window into what occurred during the course, highlights what worked and what did not, and showcases the student learning that resulted. By documenting your classroom inquiry in a portfolio and then archiving an electronic version of it on a web site (e.g., www.courseportfolio.org), you make your inquiry available to be shared, used, and reviewed by other teachers and students. For example, one teacher shared her course portfolio with other teachers across the state who taught a similar course. At the same time, she directed her students to the site so that they could see her rationale for her course objectives and assignments. Such an approach offers you the opportunity for low-stakes external feedback and commentary.

Finally, you can develop your inquiry for publication. Exhibit 11.3 lists several of the major scholarship of teaching and learning journals. While this listing is not exhaustive, it does highlight a range of outlets that might be appropriate places to publish your scholarly inquiry. Exhibit 11.4 offers links to numerous school web sites that provide detailed lists of discipline-specific teaching journals (including online or electronic journals) that might be yet another venue for publishing your work.

EXHIBIT 11.3

Examples of Scholarship of Teaching and Learning Journals

- *International Journal for the Scholarship of Teaching and Learning*
  www.georgiasouthern.edu/ijsotl
- *MountainRise*
  mountainrise.wcu.edu
- *International Journal of Teaching and Learning in Higher Education*
  www.isetl.org/ijtlhe/
- *Journal of Scholarship of Teaching and Learning*
  www.iupui.edu/~josotl/
- *Active Learning in Higher Education*
  alh.sagepub.com/
- *Academic Exchange Quarterly*
  www.rapidintellect.com/AEQweb/
- *inventio*
  www.doiiit.gmu.edu/inventio

EXHIBIT 11.4

Links to Lists of Discipline-Specific Teaching Journals

- Illinois State University
  www.ilstu.edu/~sknaylor/sotl.htm
- Indiana University–Bloomington
  www.libraries.iub.edu/index.php?pageId=438
- University of Illinois at Urbana-Champaign
  www.oir.uiuc.edu/did/Resources/Journals.htm
- Abilene Christian University
  www.acu.edu/academics/library/sotl.html
- Youngstown State University
  www.ysu.edu/catalyst/journals.htm
- University of Wisconsin-Milwaukee
  www4.uwm.edu/LeadershipSite/publicationsoutlets.cfm
- Missouri State University
  adc.missouristate.edu/SoTLJournals.htm
- Georgetown University
  crossroads.georgetown.edu/vkp/resources/journals.htm

- Buffalo State University
  www.buffalostate.edu/orgs/castl/publish.html
- Kansas State University
  www.idea.ksu.edu/papers/Idea_Paper_28.pdf

RESOURCES FOR LEARNING MORE

We hope that you find this book to be a valuable resource, but it is no substitute for discussions with others who care about teaching. One of the best resources you may have for focused guidance as you carry out your classroom inquiry is your school's teaching and learning center. Other common names for this faculty professional development office are Center for Teaching Excellence, Center for Faculty Development, and Campus Instructional Consulting. Teachers sometimes have the perception that they should make use of this resource only when they have a "problem" that needs to be fixed, but this is a misperception. Most centers have knowledgeable and skilled staff who can help guide you with your classroom inquiry. Exhibit 11.5 lists ways that they can assist you.

EXHIBIT 11.5
Issues for Which a Teaching and Learning Center Can Help

- Formulating a research question
- Sharing prior work done on the research question
- Offering feedback on your plan for collecting data and evidence
- Providing guidance on developing documentation procedures, student consent forms, or other supporting materials
- Helping you interpret your data and understand its implications for your teaching
- Helping you identify a means for sharing or disseminating your results
- Identifying others who might want to collaborate with you and extend your work beyond your particular course

---

Beyond your own school's resources, you can connect with several national organizations and major projects that focus on issues of classroom inquiry and student learning. Reviewing the work produced within these various networks can provide you with ideas for your own inquiry as well as link you with others who are interested in similar issues. Some of the major organizations and projects include:

- *International Society for the Scholarship of Teaching and Learning* (ISSOTL) (www.issotl.org/index.html). The goal of ISSOTL is to foster inquiry and disseminate findings about what improves post-secondary learning and teaching.
- *Carnegie Foundation for the Advancement of Teaching* (www.carnegiefoundation.org). Founded in 1905, the foundation is a major national and international center for research and policy studies about teaching.
- *Carnegie Academy for the Scholarship of Teaching and Learning (CASTL) Higher Education Program* (www.carnegiefoundation.org/castl). CASTL seeks to support the development of a scholarship of teaching and learning that 1) fosters significant, long-lasting learning for all students; 2) enhances the practice and profession of teaching; and 3) brings faculty members' work as teachers the recognition and reward afforded to other forms of scholarly work.
- *Peer Review of Teaching Project* (www.courseportfolio.org). Based at the University of Nebraska–Lincoln, the project supports developing a campus climate for teaching improvement and reform. The project hosts an electronic repository with more than 250 course portfolios written by faculty from around the world who teach at postsecondary institutions. Beyond reading about other classroom inquiry, visitors to the site also can write review comments to be sent to course portfolio authors.
- *Visible Knowledge Project* (crossroads.georgetown.edu/vkp/). Directed out of Georgetown University, the project aims to improve the quality of college and university teaching through a focus on both student learning and faculty development in technology-enhanced environments. The project has been instrumental in introducing virtual posters that highlight faculty inquiry efforts.

Besides these national organizations, Hakim (2002) has compiled an extensive online list of resources, articles, and reports. Exhibit 11.6 lists three additional resources to help those who wish to become involved with the scholarship of teaching and learning. The first two provide examples and descriptions of working with an institutional review board for human subjects. The last resource lists potential foundations and agencies that could help fund your classroom inquiry work.

EXHIBIT 11.6
Links to IRB and Funding Information

Institutional Review Board for Human Subject Research
- Georgetown University
  crossroads.georgetown.edu/vkp/resources/kits/irb/index.htm
- Indiana University–Bloomington
  www.indiana.edu/~sotl/humansub.html

Potential Funding Sources
- University of Illinois at Urbana-Champaign
  www.oir.uiuc.edu/did/SOTL/Funding.htm

AN INVITATION TO SET OUT ON YOUR SCHOLARLY JOURNEY

We hope that the inquiry model and the examples in this book have given you some concrete ideas about how to begin a scholarly teaching journey. In our experience, teachers who engage in classroom inquiry often find the same joy of inquiry in their teaching that they already experience in other areas of their intellectual life. Oftentimes conducting a classroom inquiry project can have a transformative impact on a teacher. Consider this comment from a professor of industrial engineering:

> I have always been a good teacher. My classroom inquiry work has allowed me to become better as I have developed the means to continue and measure the impact of course changes on my students' learning. As I have become more articulate about the criteria for improved student performance, I have successfully challenged my students to become more responsible for and involved in their own learning.

We encourage you to borrow and adapt the ideas we have presented here as you incorporate classroom inquiry into your teaching. As you map your own journey as a scholarly teacher, regardless of which path you pursue, you can be sure that it will open new vistas and bring many rewards.

BIBLIOGRAPHY

Angelo, T. A., & Cross, K. P. (1993). *Classroom assessment techniques: A handbook for college teachers* (2nd ed.). San Francisco, CA: Jossey-Bass.

Bass, R. (1999, February). The scholarship of teaching: What's the problem? *Inventio, 1*(1). Retrieved December 17, 2006, from the George Mason University, Division of Instructional Technology web site: www.doit.gmu.edu/Archives/feb98/randybass.htm

Bennett, C. D. (2001). The scholarship of teaching and learning: A beginners view. In W. Cerbin (Ed.), *A brief guide to classroom inquiry: Version 1.0* (pp. 21–22). Retrieved December 17, 2006, from the University of Wisconsin–La Crosse, Scholarship of Teaching and Learning web site: www.uwlax.edu/sotl/subpages/briefguideversion1.pdf

Bernstein, D., Burnett, A. N., Goodburn, A., & Savory, P. (2006). *Making teaching and learning visible: Course portfolios and the peer review of teaching.* Bolton, MA: Anker.

Boyer, E. L. (1990). *Scholarship reconsidered: Priorities of the professoriate.* Princeton, NJ: Carnegie Foundation for the Advancement of Teaching.

Brookfield, S. D. (1995). *Becoming a critically reflective teacher.* San Francisco, CA: Jossey-Bass.

Cerbin, B., & Kopp, B. (2004). *The classroom inquiry cycle: An online tutorial.* Retrieved December 17, 2006, from the University of Wisconsin–La Crosse, Scholarship of Teaching and Learning web site: www.uwlax.edu/sotl/tutorial/contents.htm

Cross, K. P., & Steadman, M. H. (1996). *Classroom research: Implementing the scholarship of teaching.* San Francisco, CA: Jossey-Bass.

Diamond, R. M. (1989). *Designing and improving courses and curricula in higher education: A systematic approach.* San Francisco, CA: Jossey-Bass.

Edwards, B. (1999). *The new drawing on the right side of the brain: A course in enhancing creativity and artistic confidence.* New York, NY: Tarcher/Penguin.

Glassick, C. E., Huber, M. T., & Maeroff, G. I. (1997). *Scholarship assessed: Evaluation of the professoriate.* San Francisco, CA: Jossey-Bass.

Hakim, M. A. (2002, July/August). Navigating the web of discourse on the scholarship of teaching and learning: An annotated webliography. *C&RL News, 63*(1). Retrieved December 17, 2006, from www.ala.org/ala/acrl/acrlpubs/crlnews/backissues2002/julyaugust/scholarshipteaching.htm

Jones, E. E., & Gerard, H. B. (1967). *Foundations of social psychology.* New York, NY: John Wiley & Sons.

McIntosh, P. (1988). *White privilege: Unpacking the invisible knapsack.* Retrieved December 17, 2006, from the Arizona State University web site: http://seamonkey.ed.asu.edu/~mcisaac/emc598ge/Unpacking.html

Shulman, L. S. (1998). Course anatomy: The dissection and analysis of knowledge through teaching. In P. Hutchings (Ed.), *The course portfolio: How faculty can examine their teaching to advance practice and improve student learning* (pp. 5–12). Sterling, VA: Stylus.

Walvoord, B. E., & Anderson, V. J. (1998). *Effective grading: A tool for learning and assessment.* San Francisco, CA: Jossey-Bass.

Wandt, E. (1981). Form for the evaluation of an article. In S. Isaac & W. Michael, *Handbook in research and evaluation: A collection of principles, methods, and strategies* (2nd ed., p. 220). San Diego: CA: Edits.

INDEX